READ AND SHARE

LOOK, I'M READING!

Bible

STORYBOOK

To:

_____

From:

_____

Date:

_____

Read and Share Look, I'm Reading! Bible Storybook

© 2016 by Thomas Nelson

Published in Nashville, Tennessee, by Tommy Nelson. Tommy Nelson is an imprint of Thomas Nelson. Thomas Nelson is a registered trademark of HarperCollins Christian Publishing, Inc.

Stories retold by Gwen Ellis

Illustrated by Steve Smallman

Tommy Nelson titles may be purchased in bulk for educational, business, fund-raising, or sales promotional use. For information, please e-mail SpecialMarkets@ThomasNelson.com.

Stories based on the International Children's Bible®. Copyright © 1986, 1988, 1999 by Thomas Nelson. Used by permission. All rights reserved.

ISBN-13: 978-0-7180-8869-9

Library of Congress Cataloging-in-Publication Data is on file.

Printed in China
16 17 18 19 20 DSC 5 4 3 2 1

Mfr: DSC / Shenzhen, China / October 2016 / PO # 9400925

READ AND SHARE

LOOK, I'M READING!

Bible

STORYBOOK

Stories Retold
by Gwen Ellis

Illustrated by
Steve Smallman

Tommy NELSON

A Division of Thomas Nelson Publishers

Tips for Using This Book

What you are holding in your hands is not just a book; it's a unique way to share God's Word with the little ones in your life, a way to help them come to know God's love and goodness . . . even before they can read independently! These tips will help keep young children engaged as they help you tell each story.

- Read these stories aloud to your children. Dramatize the story as you read. Kids will love it, listen, respond, and remember.

- Before you begin each Bible story, look at the picture key. Point to each picture and tell your children what word each picture represents. Younger children may be able to learn just one word, while older children may be able to remember all three.

- As you're reading and come to a picture, point to the picture to prompt your children to say the word the picture represents. If the picture represents *lake* and they say *water*, that's okay! Feel free to adapt as needed for your children's learning levels.

- When the Bible story is over, help your children focus on the real meaning of the story. Each has a Scripture reference to make it easy for you to read more about the story from the Bible.

Contents

Old Testament Stories

The Beginning
The First Day   Genesis 1:1–5   2
The Second Day   Genesis 1:6–8   4
The Third Day   Genesis 1:9–13   6
The Fourth Day   Genesis 1:14–19   8
The Fifth Day   Genesis 1:20–23   10
The Sixth Day   Genesis 1:24–31   12
Adam and Eve   Genesis 2:1–5, 15–22; 3:20   14
The Sneaky Snake   Genesis 2:16–17; 3:1–6   16
Out of the Garden   Genesis 3:8–24   18

The Flood
Noah   Genesis 6   20
The Big Boat   Genesis 7:1–15   22
Inside the Boat   Genesis 7:16–24   24
The Dove   Genesis 7:12; 8:1–19   26
The Rainbow   Genesis 8:18–22; 9:1–17   28

Abraham's Family
Abram   Genesis 12:1–3; 15:5; 22:17   30
Promised Land   Genesis 12:1–9   32
Abraham's Visitors   Genesis 17:1–8; 18:1–8   34
Sarah Laughs   Genesis 18:9–16   36
Baby Isaac   Genesis 21:1–7   38
Joseph's Coat   Genesis 37:3, 12–20   40
Joseph Is Sold   Genesis 37:21–28   42
Joseph the Slave   Genesis 39:1–6   44
Joseph in Jail   Genesis 39:6–20   46

Joseph Explains Dreams	Genesis 40:1–13, 20–21	48
The King's Dream	Genesis 41:1–36	50
Joseph in Charge	Genesis 41:37–43	52
Joseph's Brothers Visit Egypt	Genesis 41:46–42:6	54
Jacob Goes to Egypt	Genesis 44:3–45:28	56

Moses
A Mean King	Exodus 1:8–14	58
A Baby Boy	Exodus 1:22–2:2	60
The Good Sister	Exodus 2:3–4	62
A Princess Finds Moses	Exodus 2:5–10	64
Moses' Mother Helps	Exodus 2:7–10	66
Strange Fire	Exodus 3:4–12	68
Moses Goes Home	Exodus 4:14–5:1	70
The King Says No!	Exodus 5:1–9, 20–21	72
Something Awful	Exodus 12:29–51	74
Cloud and Fire	Exodus 13:21–22	76
Trapped at the Red Sea	Exodus 14:5–14	78
A Dry Path	Exodus 14:15–31	80
Food and Water	Exodus 15:22–17:7	82
Ten Commandments	Exodus 20:2–17; 24:12–18	84
Twelve Men Explore	Numbers 13:1–14:35	86

The Promised Land
Crossing the Jordan	Joshua 3	88
The Walls of Jericho	Joshua 6	90

Ruth and Naomi
Ruth and Naomi	Ruth 1	92
Ruth Gathers Grain	Ruth 2	94
Ruth and Boaz	Ruth 3–4	96

David
The Youngest Son	1 Samuel 16:1–13	98
David and the Giant	1 Samuel 17:1–24	100
Down Goes the Giant	1 Samuel 17:25–58	102

God's People Made Slaves
Captured!   2 Kings 24:18–25:21;
                                     2 Chronicles 36:15–23   104

Esther
Beautiful Queen Esther   Esther 1–3   106
Esther Saves Her People   Esther 4–9   108

Jonah
Jonah Runs Away   Jonah 1:1–3   110
A Big Storm!   Jonah 1:4–6   112
Jonah Goes Overboard   Jonah 1:7–16   114
Inside a Big Fish!   Jonah 1:17–2:9   116
Jonah Obeys God   Jonah 2:10–3:10   118

New Testament Stories

Jesus Is Born
An Angel's Message   Luke 1:5–20   122
A Baby Named John   Luke 1:57–66   124
Mary's Big Surprise   Luke 1:26–38   126
Joseph Marries Mary   Matthew 1:18–25   128
God's Baby Son   Luke 2:1–7   130
Some Sleepy Shepherds   Luke 2:8–12   132
What the Shepherds Saw   Luke 2:13–20   134
Gifts for Baby Jesus   Matthew 2:1–12   136

John the Baptist
The Man Who Ate Locusts   Matthew 3:1–13; Mark 1:4–9   138
John Baptizes Jesus   Matthew 3:13–17   140

Jesus' Life

A Little Boy Helps Jesus	John 6:1–13	142
Jesus Stops a Storm	Mark 4:35–41	144
A Very Poor Woman	Mark 12:41–44	146
One Lost Sheep	Luke 15:3–7	148

Jesus' Death and Resurrection

The First Lord's Supper	Matthew 26:26–29; 1 Corinthians 11:23–25	150
Jesus Prays for Help	Matthew 26:36–40; Mark 14:32–42; Luke 22:39–46	152
Jesus Is Arrested	Matthew 26:45–56; Luke 22:45–51; John 18:10–11	154
Pilate Questions Jesus	Luke 22:52–23:25	156
Jesus Is Killed on a Cross	Matthew 27:27–40; Mark 15:25–27	158
A Dark Day	Matthew 27:45–54; Luke 23:44–49; Hebrews 9	160
Jesus Is Laid in a Tomb	Luke 23:50–56	162
A Big Surprise	Matthew 28:1–10	164
Jesus Is Alive!	Matthew 28:5–8; Luke 24:9–12	166
Jesus Appears to a Room Full of Friends	Luke 24:36–49	168
Jesus Goes to Heaven	Luke 24:50–53; Acts 1:6–11	170

The Holy Spirit Comes

God's Spirit Comes to Help	Acts 2:1–4	172

Saul Becomes Paul

A Mean Man	Acts 9:1–4	174
Saul Is Blinded	Acts 9:4–9	176
Ananias Helps Saul	Acts 9:10–18; 13:9	178

Peter

Peter in Jail	Acts 12:1–18	180

The Best Is Yet to Come

New Heaven and Earth	Revelation 21	182

Old Testament Stories

The First Day

Genesis 1:1–5

earth   day   night

In the beginning God made heaven and ⬤.
At first it was empty and dark. But God
gathered up the light and called it ☀.

   Then He gathered up the darkness and
called it 🌙. God was watching over
everything.

The Second Day

Genesis 1:6–8

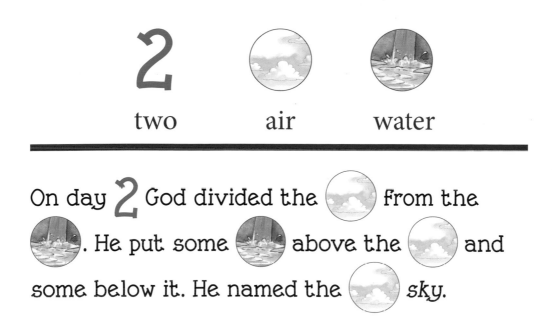

2 two · air · water

On day 2 God divided the from the . He put some above the and some below it. He named the sky.

The Third Day

Genesis 1:9–13

On day 3 God was busy. He used  to make puddles and oceans and lakes and waterfalls and rivers. He made the dry ground too.

Next He made 🌼. He made so many different kinds of trees, flowers, and bushes that no one could count all the 🌼. God said His work was good.

The Fourth Day

Genesis 1:14–19

8

4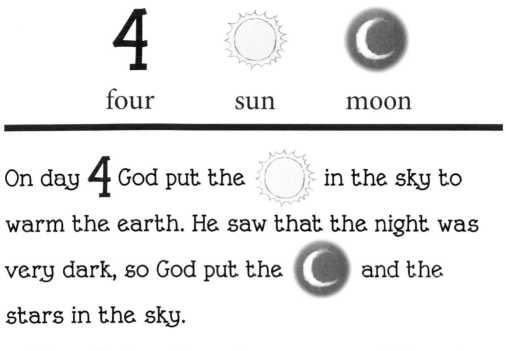

four   sun   moon

On day **4** God put the ☀ in the sky to warm the earth. He saw that the night was very dark, so God put the 🌙 and the stars in the sky.

Then God made spring, summer, fall, and winter. All that He made was good.

The Fifth Day

Genesis 1:20–23

five   fish   birds

On day 5 God made starfish, octopuses, whales, and turtles. He made fast little for rivers and slippery big for the ocean.

He made big like eagles to soar in the sky and zippy little like hummingbirds. He made in all shapes, sizes, and colors.

The Sixth Day

Genesis 1:24–31

6

six   bears   people

On day 6 God made the animals—puppies, cows, horses, kitties, , lizards, mice, worms, and lots more. Everything was good.

But something was still missing. There were no . So God made some. And when He made , He made them like Himself. He made so they could be friends with Him.

13

Adam and Eve

Adam   Eve   7 seven

God named the first man . God put  in a beautiful garden. He gave  all the animals. He gave him all the fish and the birds too.

Then God gave  one more thing. God made a woman to be 's wife.  named his wife . On day **7** God rested from all His work.

The Sneaky Snake

Genesis 2:16–17; 3:1–6

fruit   tree   snake

God gave Adam and Eve one rule: "Eat anything you like except the  from the in the middle of the garden."

A sneaky old came to Eve. "If you eat the , then you'll know everything, just like God." So Eve ate the and gave some to Adam. And he ate the too.

Out of the Garden

Genesis 3:8–24

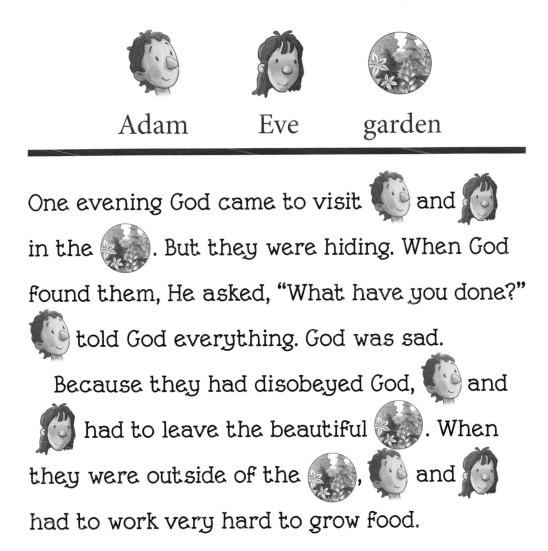

Adam   Eve   garden

One evening God came to visit and in the . But they were hiding. When God found them, He asked, "What have you done?" told God everything. God was sad.

Because they had disobeyed God, and had to leave the beautiful . When they were outside of the , and had to work very hard to grow food.

Noah

Genesis 6

earth   Noah   boat

Many years later there were lots of people

on the ⬤, but most of them were

bad. One man named 🧔 was good. He

obeyed God. "I want you to build a 🛶,"

God told 🧔.

🧔 started right away. People laughed at

him because they lived in a desert and there

was no water for his 🛶. 🧔 just went

on building the 🛶.

The Big Boat

Genesis 7:1–15

boat   Noah   animal

When the 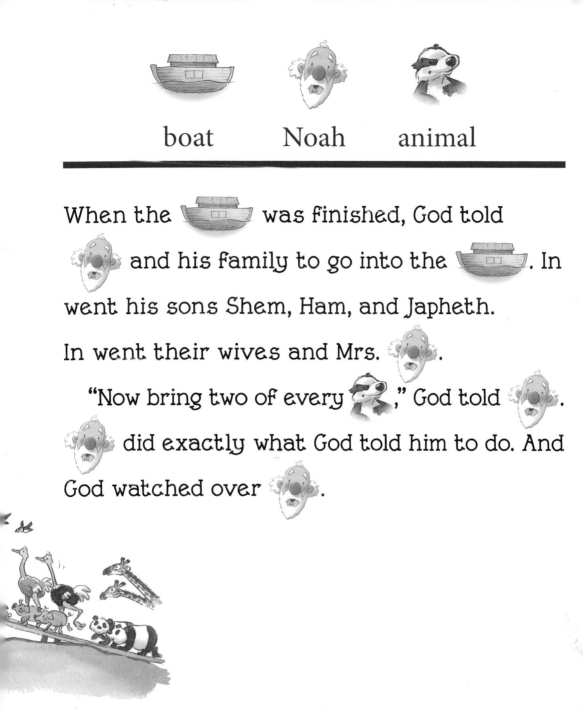 was finished, God told

and his family to go into the . In

went his sons Shem, Ham, and Japheth.

In went their wives and Mrs. .

"Now bring two of every ," God told .

did exactly what God told him to do. And

God watched over .

Inside the Boat

Genesis 7:16–24

24

boat　　　　rain　　mountains

When the last animal climbed into the ,

God shut the door. *Plip! Plop! Plip!* It began to

. There was so much , the water

was over the meadows. There was so much

, it covered the towns. There was so

much , it even covered the .

But inside the , everyone was safe.

The Dove

Genesis 7:12; 8:1–19

dove   earth   leaf

After forty days and forty nights, the rain stopped, but it still wasn't time to get off of the boat. Water was everywhere. One day Noah let a little  fly out to see what was happening on the .

The brought a green back. Hooray! The meant plants were growing again! It was almost time to come out!

The Rainbow

Genesis 8:18–22; 9:1–17

boat   Noah   rainbow

When everyone was out of the 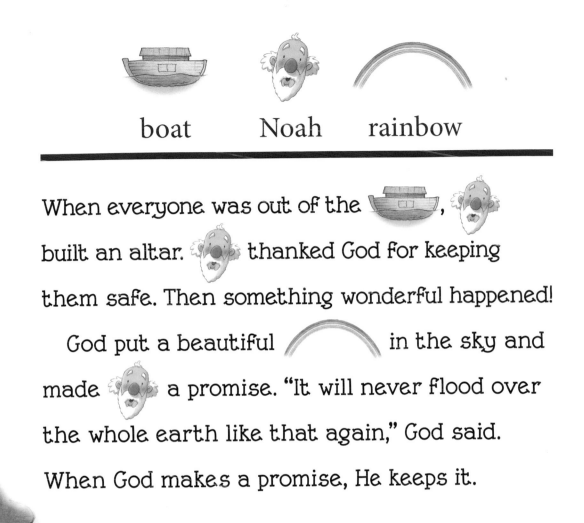,

built an altar. thanked God for keeping

them safe. Then something wonderful happened!

God put a beautiful in the sky and

made a promise. "It will never flood over

the whole earth like that again," God said.

When God makes a promise, He keeps it.

Abram

Genesis 12:1–3; 15:5; 22:17

Abram   stars   sand

God picked to be the father of a very

important family. One day in the future,

Jesus would come from 's family.

God told , "I will make you famous.

Your children and grandchildren will be

as many as the . They will be as many as

the grains of on the beach. You won't be

able to count them."

31

Promised Land

Genesis 12:1–9

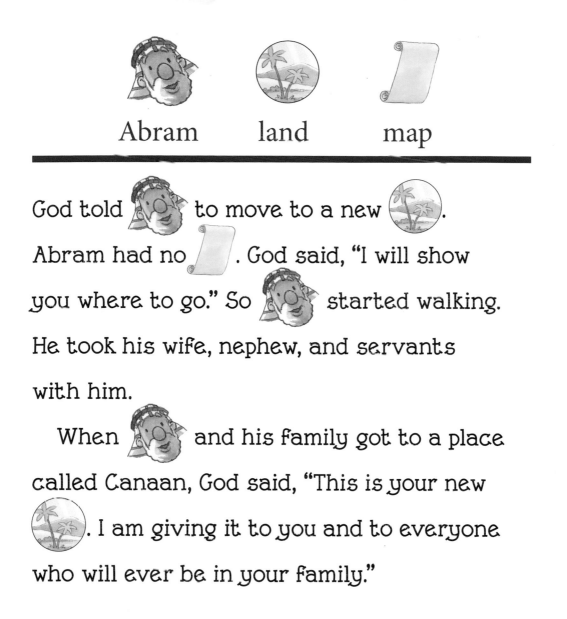

Abram   land   map

God told 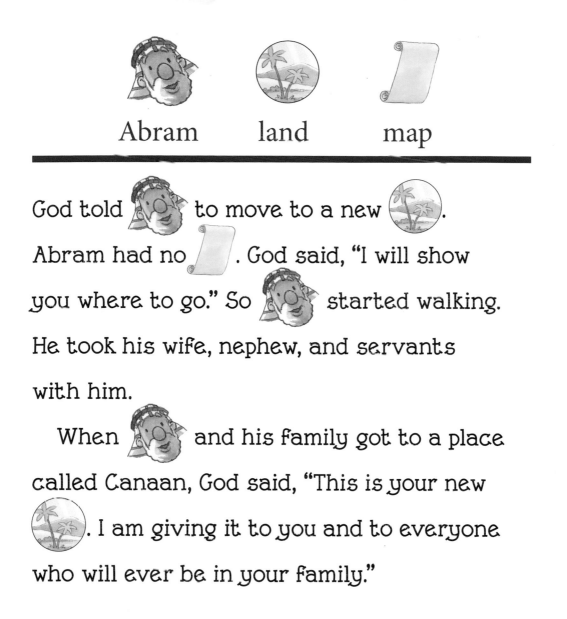 to move to a new .

Abram had no . God said, "I will show

you where to go." So started walking.

He took his wife, nephew, and servants

with him.

When and his family got to a place

called Canaan, God said, "This is your new

. I am giving it to you and to everyone

who will ever be in your family."

Abraham's Visitors

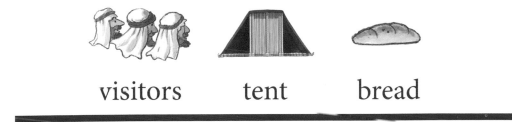

visitors   tent   bread

When Abram was ninety-nine years old, God changed his name to Abraham. His new name showed that he belonged to God. Not long after that, three came by Abraham's , and he invited them to lunch.

"Quick! Bake some ," Abraham told his wife. Then Abraham hurried to get some meat cooked. When the food was ready, Abraham brought it to his . The sat down to eat.

Sarah Laughs

Genesis 18:9–16

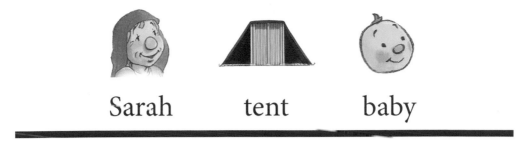

Sarah   tent   baby

When one of the visitors finished eating,

he said, "Where is your wife, ?" "She's

over there in the ," Abraham said.

"Next year will have a ," the

visitor said.

 heard and laughed. She couldn't

believe it. *I'm too old to have a* ,

thought. *Abraham is too old too.*

Baby Isaac

Genesis 21:1–7

Sarah   baby   laugh

In about a year  had a  boy, just like God had promised. Abraham named the  Isaac. Isaac means "laughter."

 was so happy with her  boy.  said, "God has made me . Everyone who hears about this will  with me."

Joseph's Coat

Genesis 37:3, 12–20

Joseph   coat   brothers

Many years later a man named Jacob had twelve sons. He loved them all, but he loved [Joseph] best. Jacob gave [Joseph] a beautiful [coat] with long sleeves. This made his [brothers] jealous. One day Jacob said, "[Joseph], go check on your [brothers]." So off [Joseph] went. His [brothers] saw him coming. "Here comes the dreamer," the [brothers] said. "Let's get rid of him." Watch out, [Joseph]!

Joseph Is Sold

Genesis 37:21–28

brothers   Joseph   slave

The 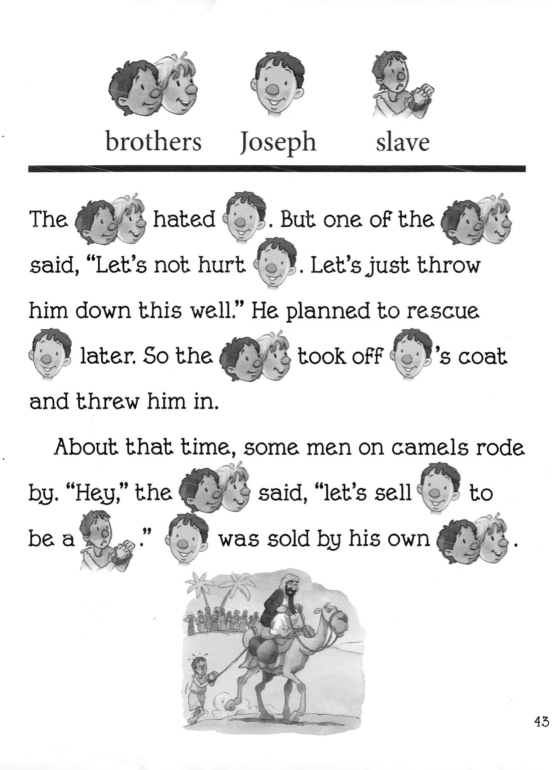 hated 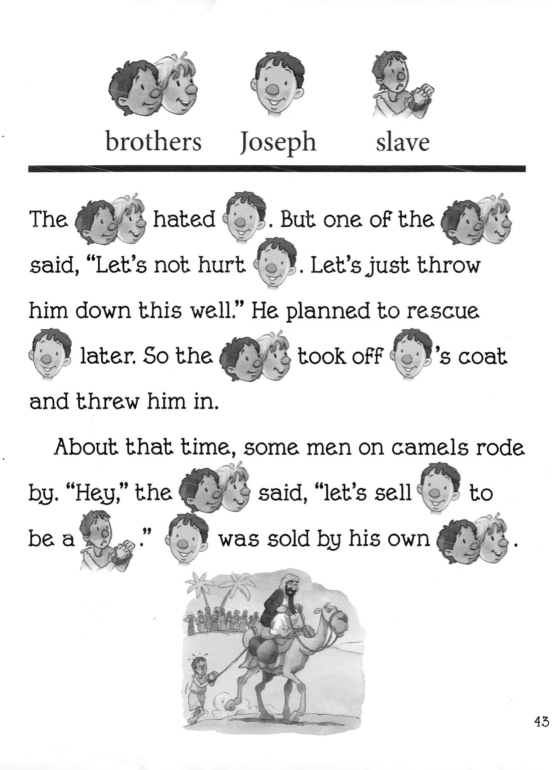. But one of the 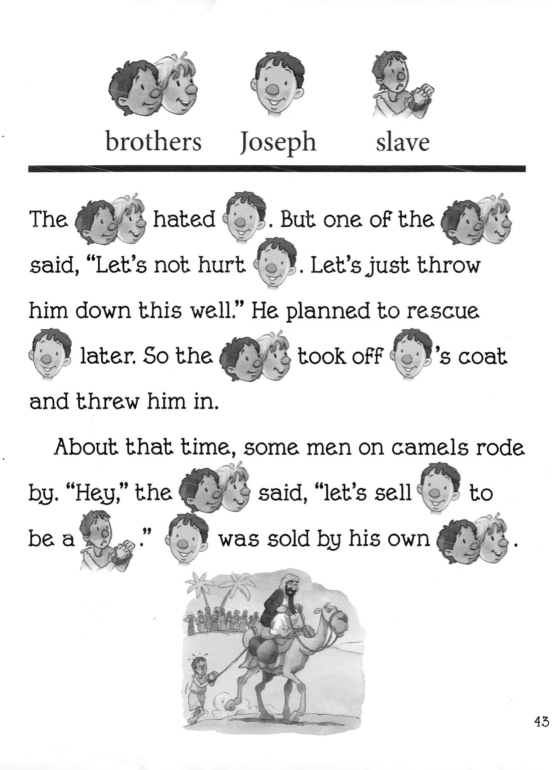 said, "Let's not hurt 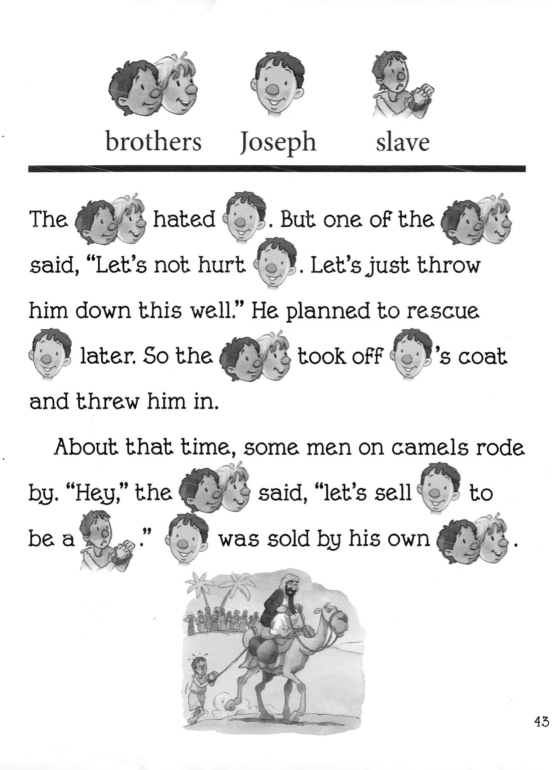. Let's just throw him down this well." He planned to rescue 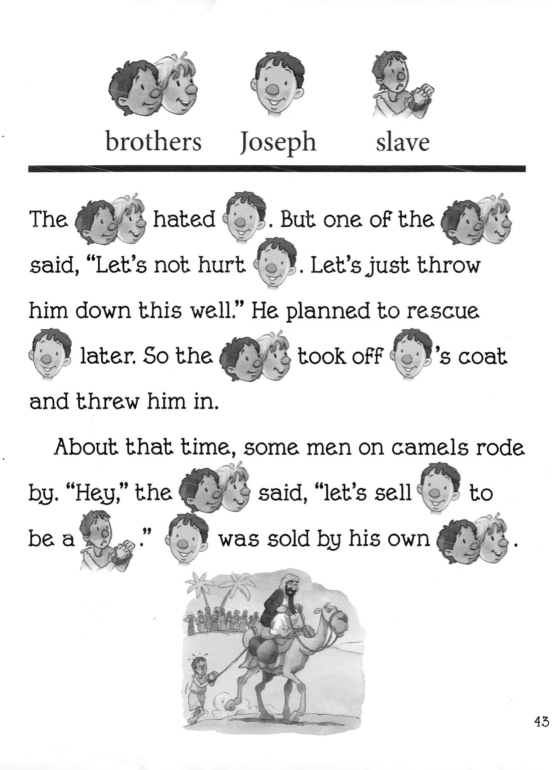 later. So the 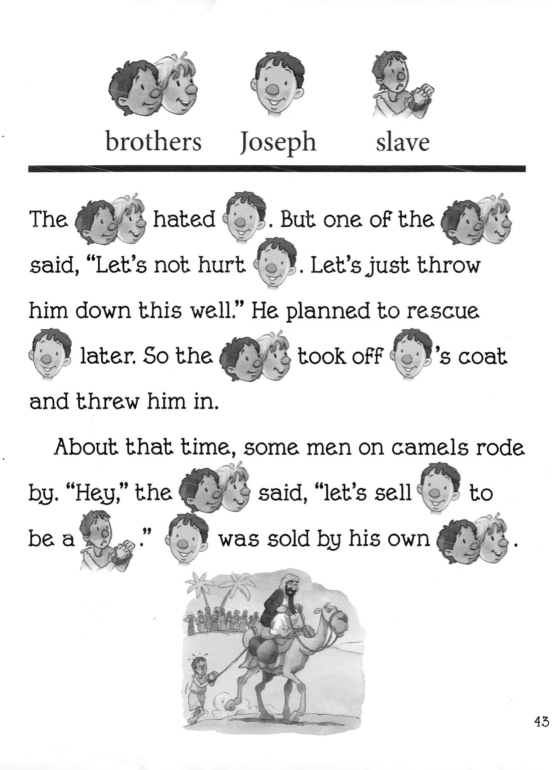 took off 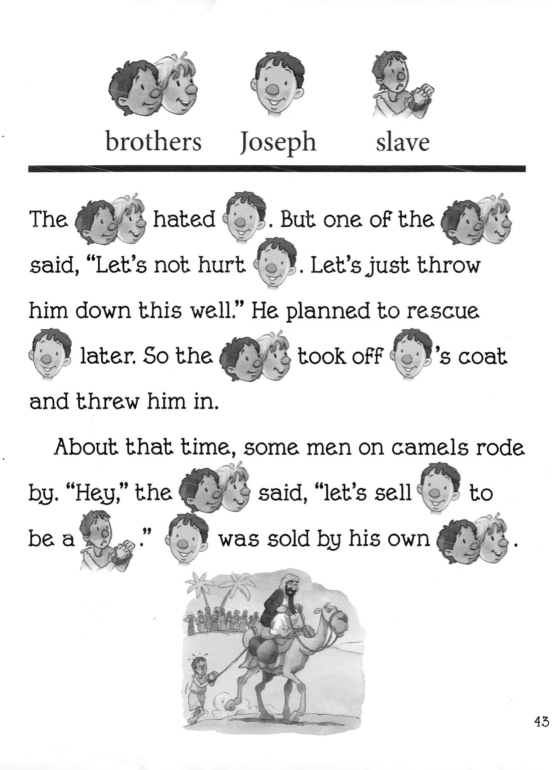's coat and threw him in.

About that time, some men on camels rode by. "Hey," the 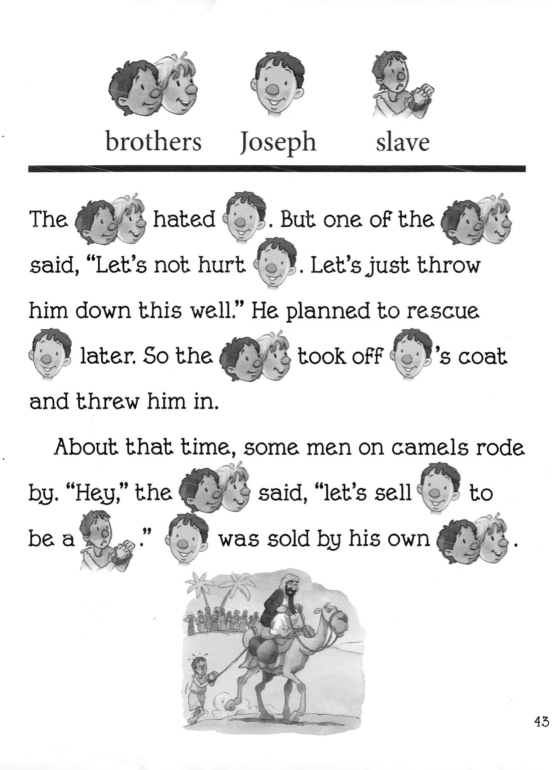 said, "let's sell 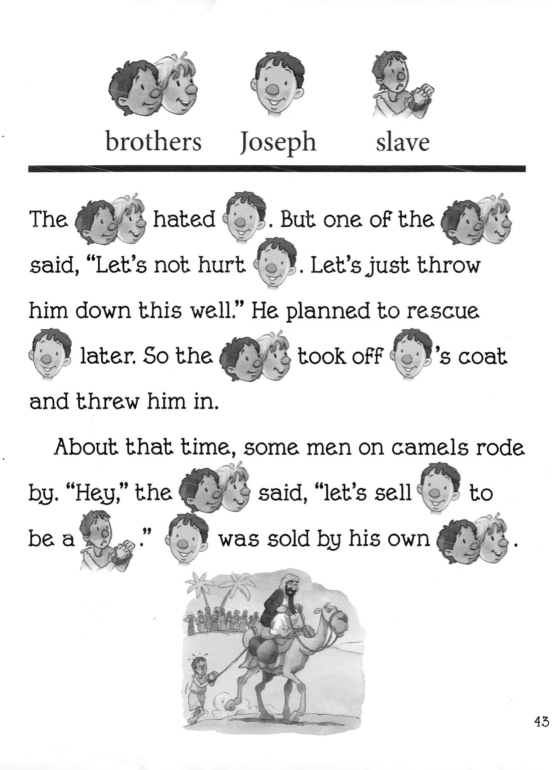 to be a 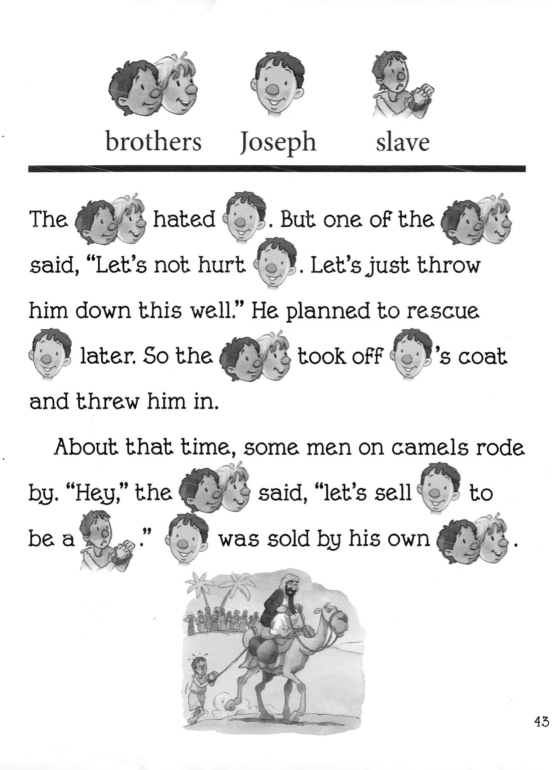." 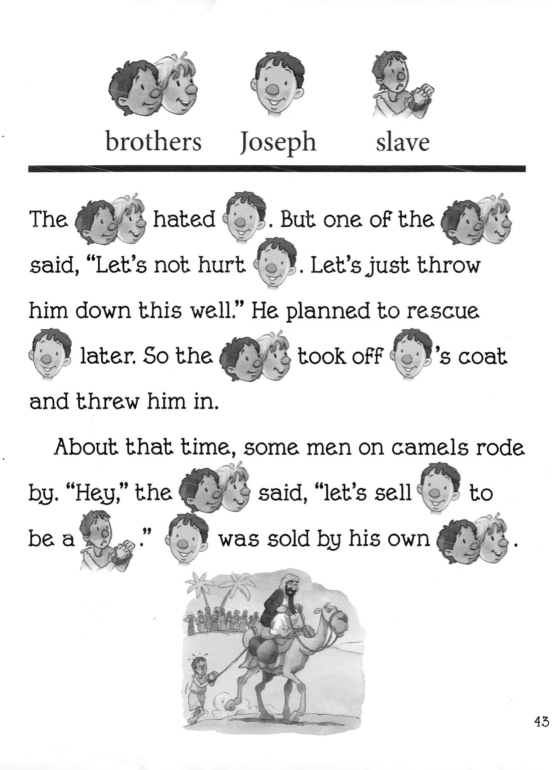 was sold by his own 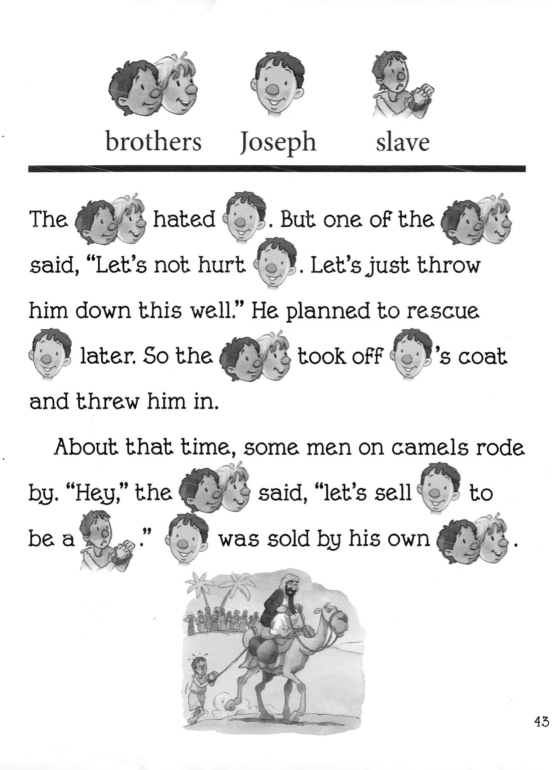.

Joseph the Slave

Genesis 39:1–6

Joseph   Potiphar   slave

Joseph was not alone. God was watching over him. Soon a rich man named Potiphar bought him to be his slave. Joseph worked and did a great job with everything Potiphar asked him to do.

So Potiphar put Joseph in charge of his whole house, and everyone had to do what Joseph said.

Joseph in Jail

Genesis 39:6–20

Joseph   wife   jail

Everything was going great for 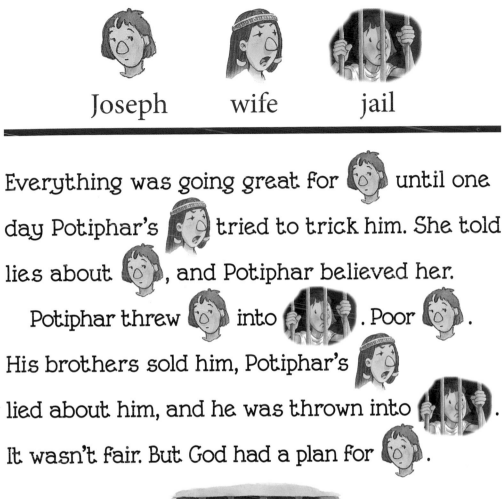 until one day Potiphar's 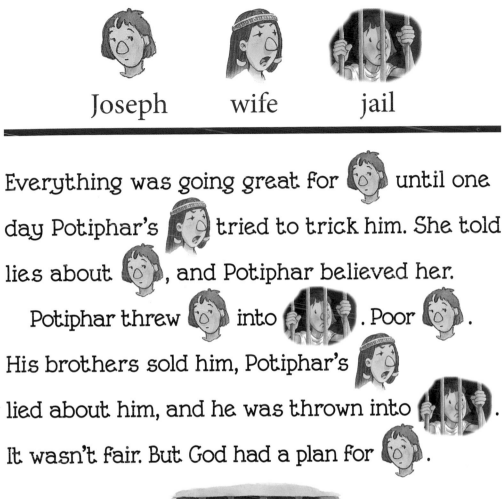 tried to trick him. She told lies about 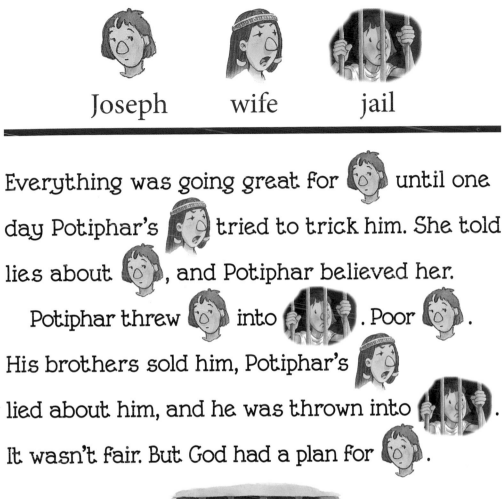, and Potiphar believed her.

Potiphar threw 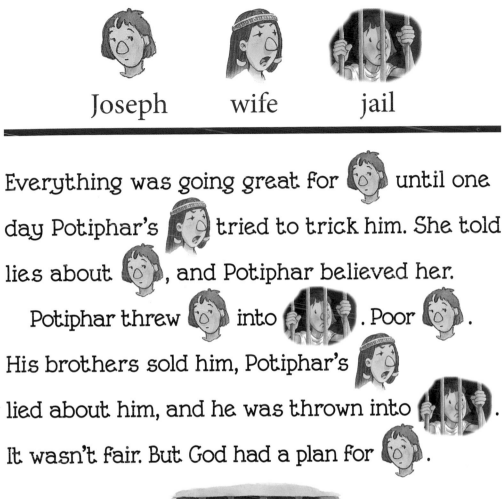 into 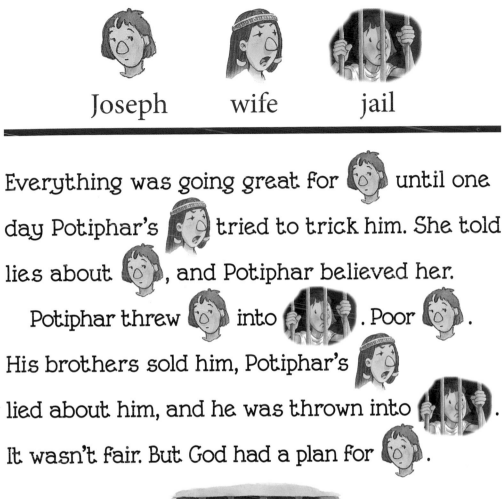. Poor 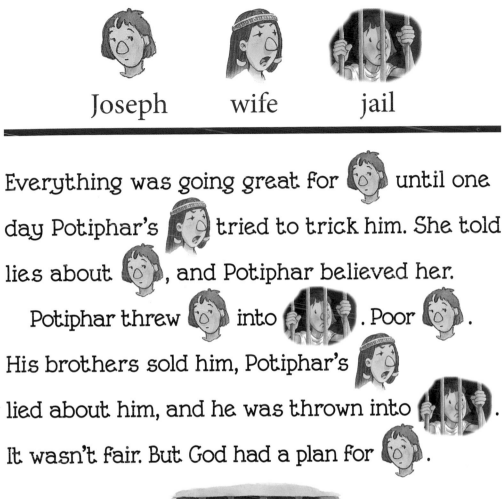. His brothers sold him, Potiphar's 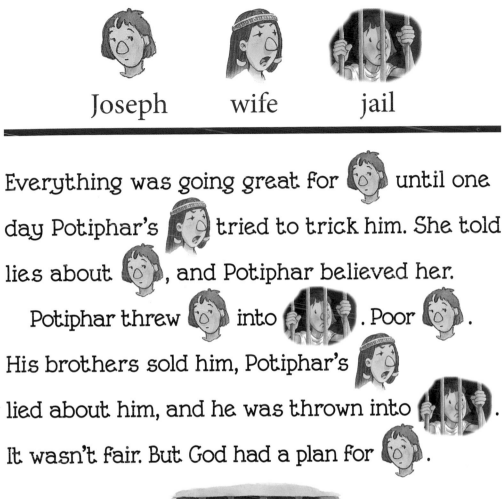 lied about him, and he was thrown into 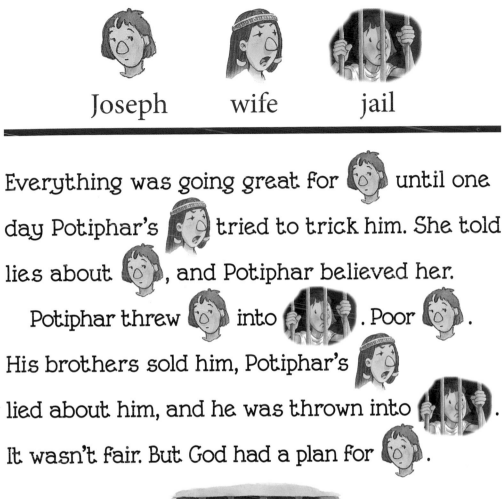. It wasn't fair. But God had a plan for 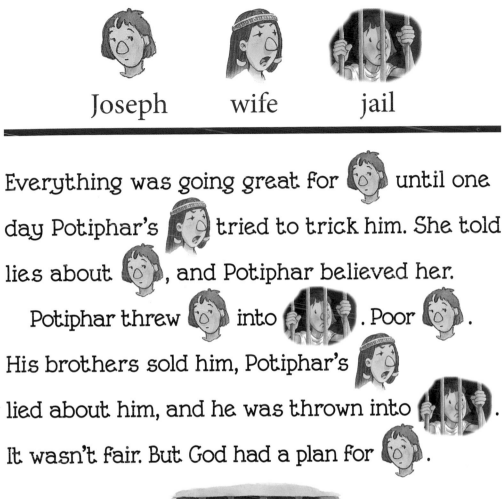.

Joseph Explains Dreams

Genesis 40:1–13, 20–21

jail   man   king

In the 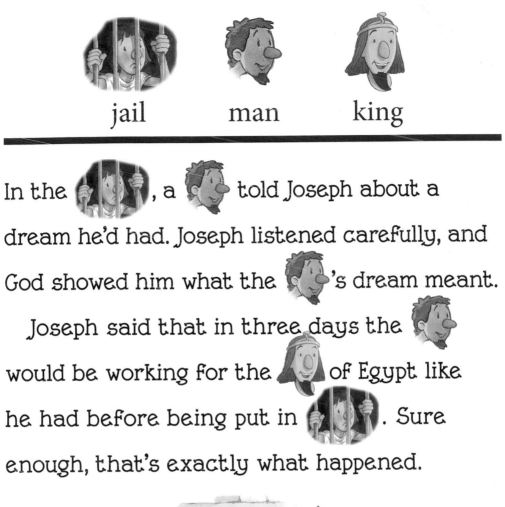, a told Joseph about a dream he'd had. Joseph listened carefully, and God showed him what the 's dream meant.

Joseph said that in three days the would be working for the of Egypt like he had before being put in . Sure enough, that's exactly what happened.

The King's Dream

Genesis 41:1-36

king   cows   food

One night the 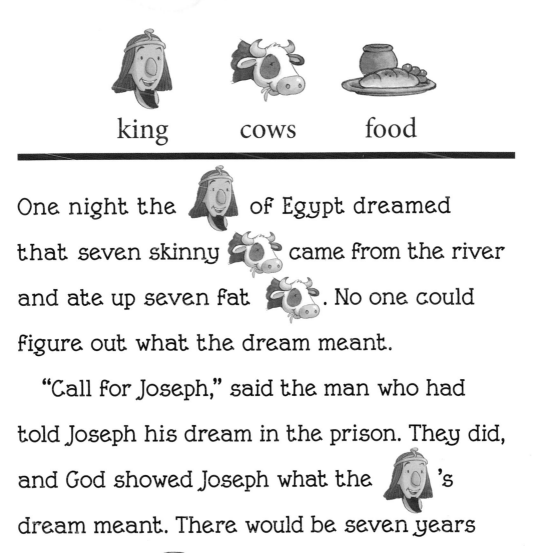 of Egypt dreamed that seven skinny cows came from the river and ate up seven fat cows. No one could figure out what the dream meant.

"Call for Joseph," said the man who had told Joseph his dream in the prison. They did, and God showed Joseph what the king's dream meant. There would be seven years with lots of food. Then there would be seven years with almost no food.

Joseph in Charge

Genesis 41:37–43

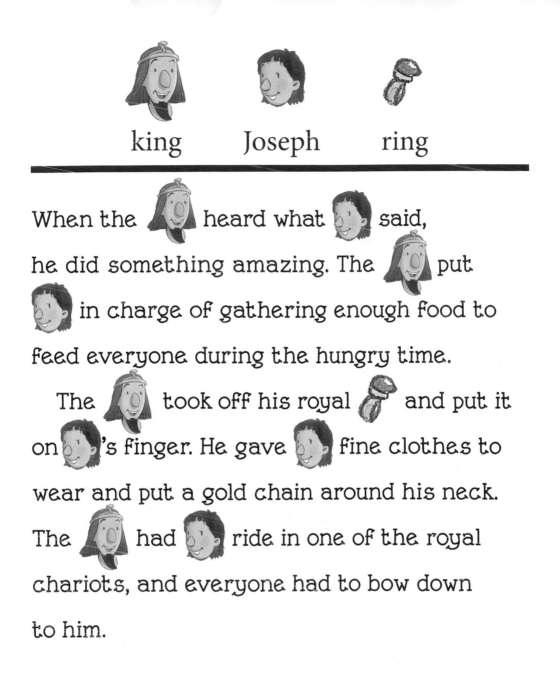

king　　　Joseph　　　ring

When the king heard what Joseph said,
he did something amazing. The king put
Joseph in charge of gathering enough food to
feed everyone during the hungry time.

The king took off his royal ring and put it
on Joseph's finger. He gave Joseph fine clothes to
wear and put a gold chain around his neck.
The king had Joseph ride in one of the royal
chariots, and everyone had to bow down
to him.

Joseph's Brothers Visit Egypt

Genesis 41:46–42:6

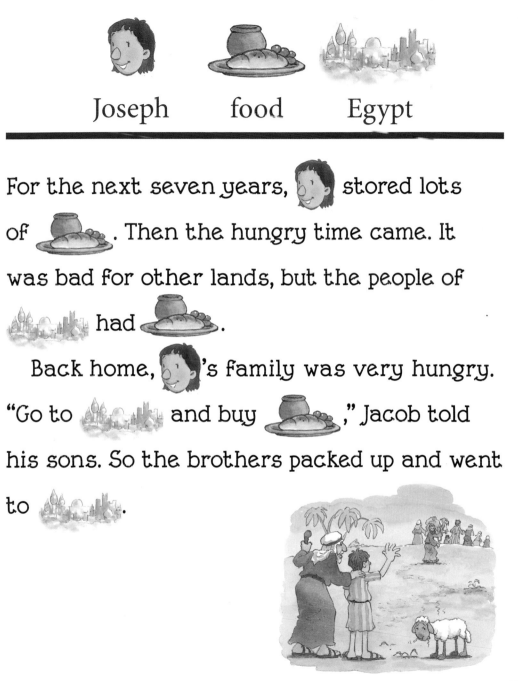

Joseph   food   Egypt

For the next seven years, stored lots of . Then the hungry time came. It was bad for other lands, but the people of had .

Back home, 's family was very hungry. "Go to and buy ," Jacob told his sons. So the brothers packed up and went to .

Jacob Goes to Egypt

Genesis 44:3–45:28

Joseph   slave   father

When the brothers came to the palace,

 knew right away who they were. But

they didn't recognize . He said, "I am

your brother . You sold me to be a

, but God sent me here to save your

lives."

"Hurry, go home and get our  and your

families and bring them here." And that's

how God's people, the Israelites, came to live

in Egypt.

A Mean King

Exodus 1:8–14

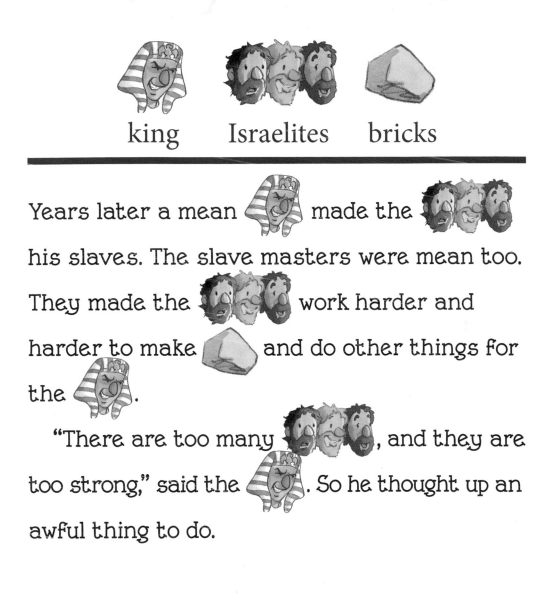

king   Israelites   bricks

Years later a mean made the his slaves. The slave masters were mean too. They made the work harder and harder to make and do other things for the .

"There are too many , and they are too strong," said the . So he thought up an awful thing to do.

A Baby Boy

Exodus 1:22–2:2

king   baby   river

That mean old  said, "Every time an Israelite  boy is born, you must throw him into the ." That was terrible!

One day an Israelite woman had a beautiful  boy. She decided to hide her  from the evil  and his helpers. It was a good plan.

The Good Sister

Exodus 2:3–4

After a while the baby's mother couldn't hide him anymore. So she got a  and fixed it so the  could not get inside.

Then she put the baby into the  and put the  into the . The baby's big , Miriam, stayed close by to see what would happen.

A Princess Finds Moses

Exodus 2:5–10

baby   princess   basket

God was watching over the . When the
 came to the river to take a bath, she
saw the . "Go get that ," she told
her servant.

The  looked inside the . Just
then the  cried, and she felt sorry for him.
The  decided to keep him as her son. She
named him Moses.

Moses' Mother Helps

Exodus 2:7–10

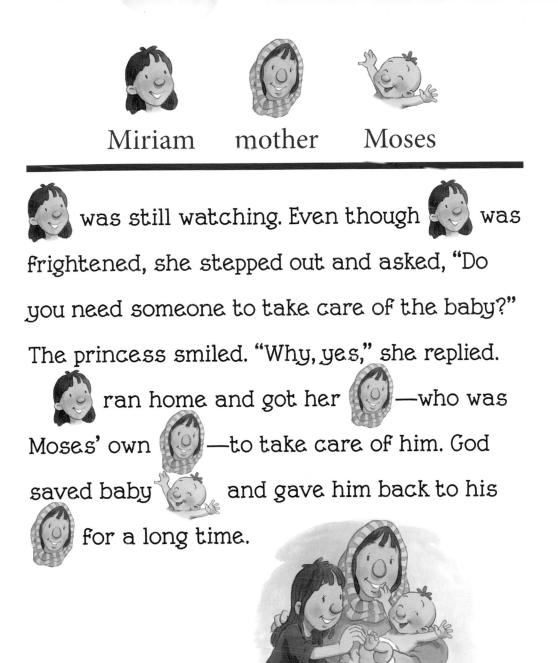

Miriam   mother   Moses

was still watching. Even though was frightened, she stepped out and asked, "Do you need someone to take care of the baby?" The princess smiled. "Why, yes," she replied.

ran home and got her —who was Moses' own —to take care of him. God saved baby and gave him back to his for a long time.

Strange Fire

Exodus 3:4–12

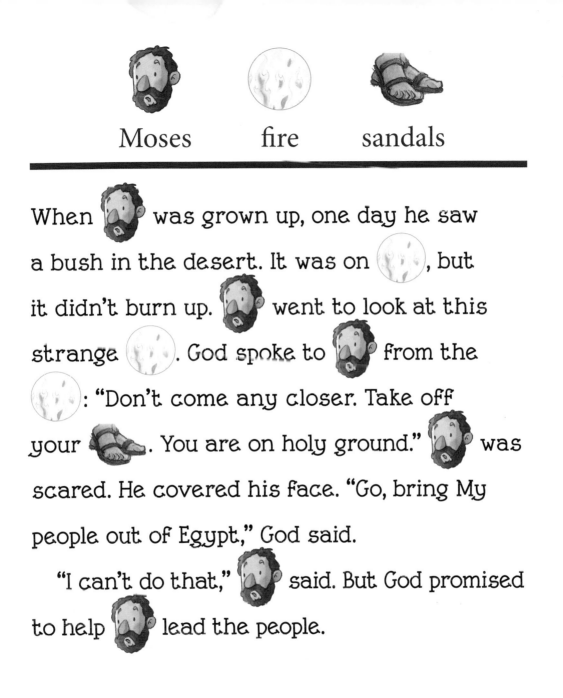

Moses   fire   sandals

When was grown up, one day he saw a bush in the desert. It was on , but it didn't burn up. went to look at this strange . God spoke to from the : "Don't come any closer. Take off your . You are on holy ground." was scared. He covered his face. "Go, bring My people out of Egypt," God said.

"I can't do that," said. But God promised to help lead the people.

Moses Goes Home

Exodus 4:14–5:1

Moses　　　Egypt　　　Aaron

went home to to talk to the Israelites about being free. God sent his brother to help him.

The Israelites fell down on their knees and thanked God for remembering them. Then it was time for to go see the mean king. took with him.

The King Says No!

Exodus 5:1–9, 20–21

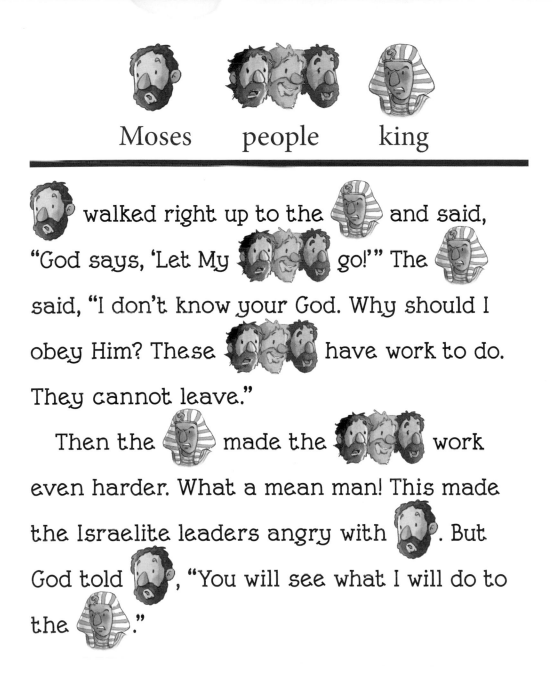

Moses   people   king

 walked right up to the and said, "God says, 'Let My go!'" The said, "I don't know your God. Why should I obey Him? These have work to do. They cannot leave."

Then the made the work even harder. What a mean man! This made the Israelite leaders angry with . But God told , "You will see what I will do to the ."

Something Awful

Exodus 12:29–51

king   animals   people

At midnight, because the 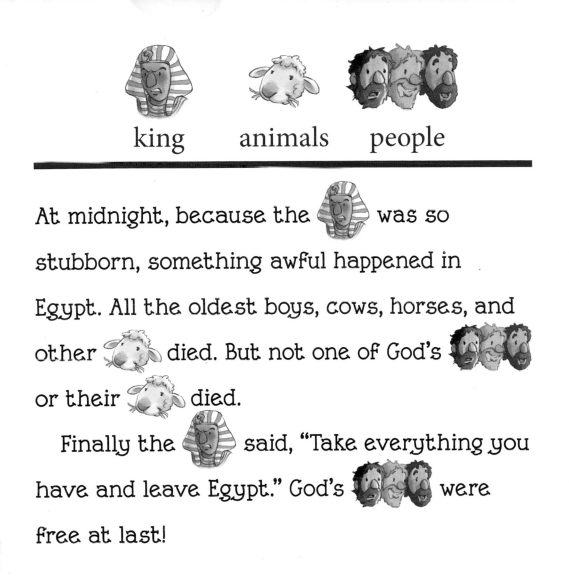 was so stubborn, something awful happened in Egypt. All the oldest boys, cows, horses, and other died. But not one of God's or their died.

Finally the said, "Take everything you have and leave Egypt." God's were free at last!

Cloud and Fire

Exodus 13:21–22

desert   cloud   fire

When God's people left Egypt, they marched

out into the . God did something very

special to help them. He sent a tall

to guide them during the day.

It was very dark in the  at night. So

God changed the  to . The  was

like a giant night-light. Now God's people could

travel some during the day and some at night.

Trapped at the Red Sea

Exodus 14:5–14

soldiers   people   sea

Back in Egypt the king changed his mind. He sent his  after God's  to bring them back. Closer and closer the army came on their horses and chariots.

God's  stood right by the Red . There was no way across the . The king's  were behind them, and the  was in front of them. It looked as if God's  were trapped, but they weren't.

A Dry Path

Exodus 14:15–31

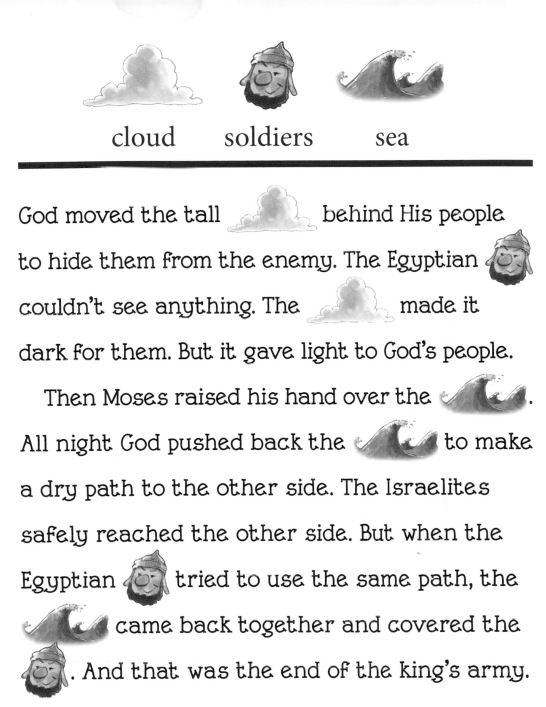

cloud   soldiers   sea

God moved the tall ☁ behind His people
to hide them from the enemy. The Egyptian 🧔
couldn't see anything. The ☁ made it
dark for them. But it gave light to God's people.

Then Moses raised his hand over the 🌊.
All night God pushed back the 🌊 to make
a dry path to the other side. The Israelites
safely reached the other side. But when the
Egyptian 🧔 tried to use the same path, the
🌊 came back together and covered the
🧔. And that was the end of the king's army.

Food and Water

Exodus 15:22–17:7

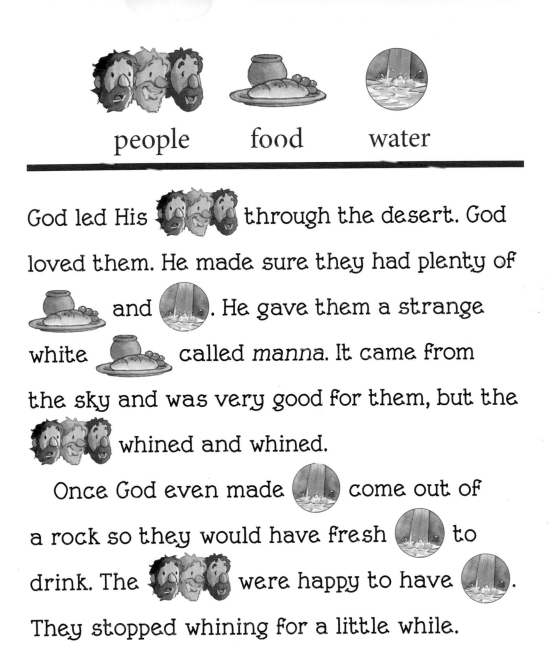

people   food   water

God led His through the desert. God loved them. He made sure they had plenty of and . He gave them a strange white called *manna*. It came from the sky and was very good for them, but the whined and whined.

Once God even made come out of a rock so they would have fresh to drink. The were happy to have . They stopped whining for a little while.

Ten Commandments

Exodus 20:2–17; 24:12–18

Moses   mountain   rules

One day God called  up to the top of a
 to have a talk.

God gave  good  to help His people
know how to live. God wrote the  on stone
with His finger. We call these  the Ten
Commandments.

Twelve Men Explore

Numbers 13:1–14:35

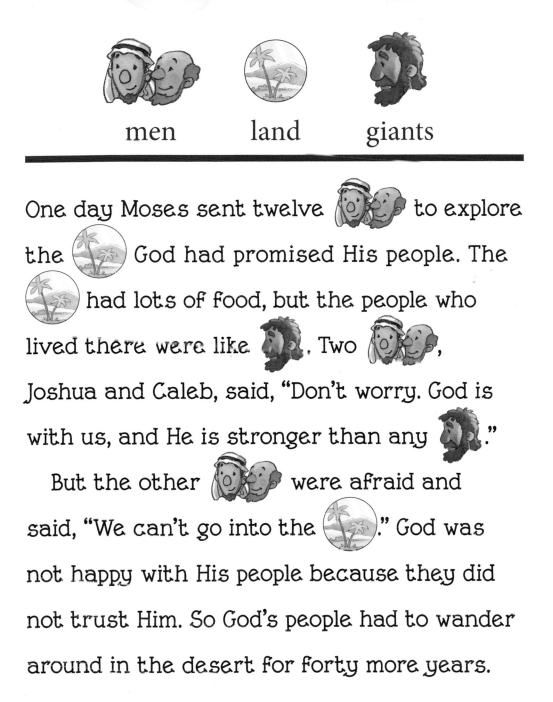

men   land   giants

One day Moses sent twelve [men] to explore

the [land] God had promised His people. The

[land] had lots of food, but the people who

lived there were like [giants]. Two [men],

Joshua and Caleb, said, "Don't worry. God is

with us, and He is stronger than any [giant]."

But the other [men] were afraid and

said, "We can't go into the [land]." God was

not happy with His people because they did

not trust Him. So God's people had to wander

around in the desert for forty more years.

Crossing the Jordan

Joshua 3

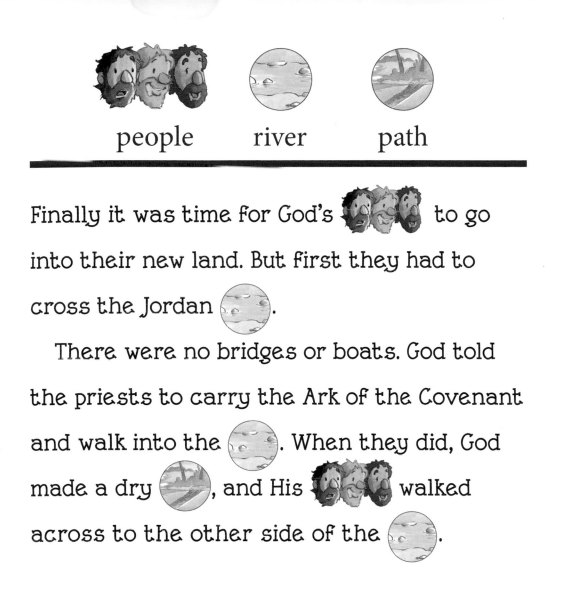

people   river   path

Finally it was time for God's to go into their new land. But first they had to cross the Jordan .

There were no bridges or boats. God told the priests to carry the Ark of the Covenant and walk into the . When they did, God made a dry , and His walked across to the other side of the .

The Walls of Jericho

Joshua 6

walls   march   trumpets

The first city God's people came to was

Jericho. It had huge  and gates and

guards everywhere. God said, " around

Jericho every day for six days. Seven priests

with  must march at the front.

"On the seventh day,  around seven

times. Then have the priests blow one long

blast on their . The people must shout,

and the  will fall down." The people

obeyed, and down came those .

Ruth and Naomi

Ruth 1

Ruth   Naomi   family

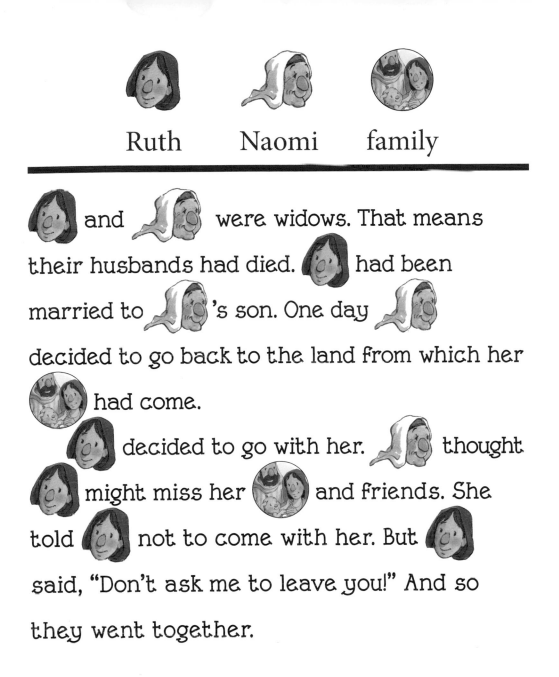

and were widows. That means their husbands had died. had been married to 's son. One day decided to go back to the land from which her had come.

 decided to go with her. thought might miss her and friends. She told not to come with her. But said, "Don't ask me to leave you!" And so they went together.

93

Ruth Gathers Grain

Ruth 2

Ruth   food   field

Ruth and Naomi were very poor. They didn't have enough food to eat. Naomi was too old to work, so Ruth went out to a rich man's field to gather leftover grain for food. The rich man saw her. "Stay here and work in my field," he told Ruth.

Ruth and Boaz

Ruth 3–4

Naomi   Boaz   Ruth

Naomi decided Boaz would be a good husband for Ruth. She told Ruth what she should do to see if Boaz wanted to marry her. Ruth did exactly what Naomi said. Boaz liked Ruth and wanted to marry her. So they were married and had a little boy.

That made all of them happy.

The Youngest Son

1 Samuel 16:1–13

sons   sheep   David

God sent Samuel to the house of a man named Jesse to choose a new king. When Samuel looked at seven of Jesse's , God said to him, "Don't look at how tall or handsome they are."

"Are these all of your ?" Samuel asked. Jesse said, "My youngest son is taking care of the . His name is ." God said to Samuel, " is the one I've chosen."

David and the Giant

1 Samuel 17:1–24

David   soldiers   Goliath

God's Holy Spirit made  brave and strong. One day Jesse told  to go check on his brothers who were . When  got to the battlefield, he found the  were all afraid of a giant named .

 liked to yell at the  and scare them.  wanted to hurt them.

Down Goes the Giant

1 Samuel 17:25–58

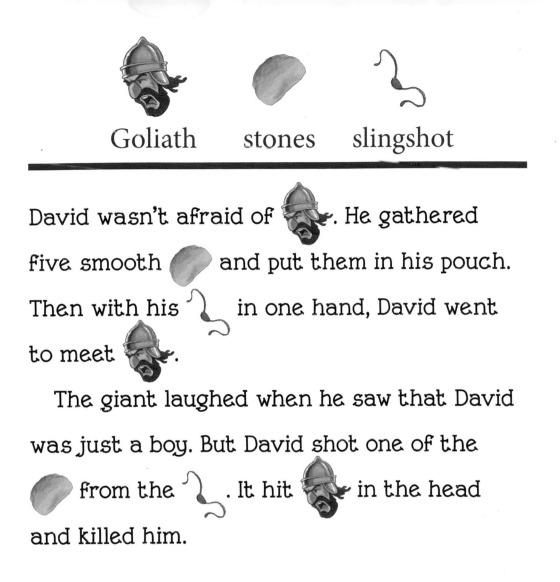

Goliath   stones   slingshot

David wasn't afraid of [Goliath]. He gathered five smooth [stones] and put them in his pouch. Then with his [slingshot] in one hand, David went to meet [Goliath].

The giant laughed when he saw that David was just a boy. But David shot one of the [stones] from the [slingshot]. It hit [Goliath] in the head and killed him.

Captured!

2 Kings 24:18–25:21; 2 Chronicles 36:15–23

people   enemy   land

Over and over God had warned His  not to worship idols. But they kept right on doing what God had told them not to do. So finally God let an  capture His  and take them from the  He'd given them. God's  were taken far away to a  called Babylon. It was a sad day.

Beautiful Queen Esther

Esther 1–3

kingdom   Esther   king

Years later the Persian  defeated

Babylon. But God's people were still living

in the land of Babylon. One of them was a

young woman named  .

The  of Persia wanted a beautiful

young woman to be his queen. He picked

 . Soon afterward one of the 's men

decided to get rid of all God's people in the

 . Since  was one of them, it

meant he would get rid of her too.

Esther Saves Her People

Esther 4–9

Esther   king   queen

 knew it was up to her to save her

people. She also knew that if she visited the

 and he got angry, she wouldn't be

anymore. The could even have

killed. What should she do?

decided to go to the anyway.

When she went, the granted her wish

that her people would be allowed to live.

Jonah Runs Away

Jonah 1:1–3

Jonah   people   ship

"Go to Nineveh," God told a man named .

"Tell the  to stop their evil ways."

 got up, but he didn't go to Nineveh.

He didn't like the  of that city, so he

ran away.

 went to the seashore. He got on a

going the opposite direction from Nineveh.

God saw what  was doing.

A Big Storm!

Jonah 1:4-6

ship   storm   waves

Jonah sailed away on the . When the was at sea, God sent a big . pounded the . The sailors were very frightened by the .

The captain went down into the bottom of the and found Jonah sleeping. "Get up and pray to your God," he said. "Maybe your God will save us!"

Jonah Goes Overboard

Jonah 1:7–16

storm   Jonah   sea

"Somebody has done something to cause

this . Let's find out who it is," the

sailors said. They decided the  was

's fault. "You're right. I ran away from

God,"  told them. "Throw me into the

. Then the  will calm down."

So the sailors tossed  overboard. As

soon as  was in the water, the

became calm.

Inside a Big Fish!

Jonah 1:17–2:9

water   Jonah   fish

Down, down into the swirling 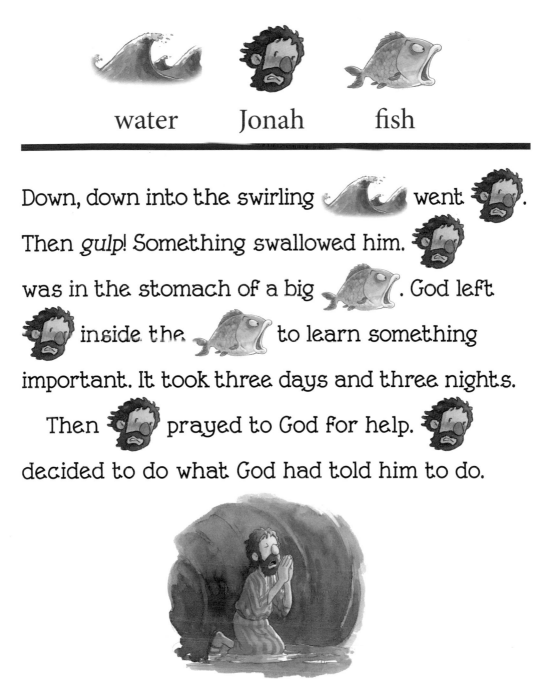 went .

Then *gulp!* Something swallowed him.

was in the stomach of a big . God left

inside the to learn something

important. It took three days and three nights.

Then prayed to God for help.

decided to do what God had told him to do.

Jonah Obeys God

Jonah 2:10–3:10

fish   beach   Jonah

God had a plan. He spoke to that 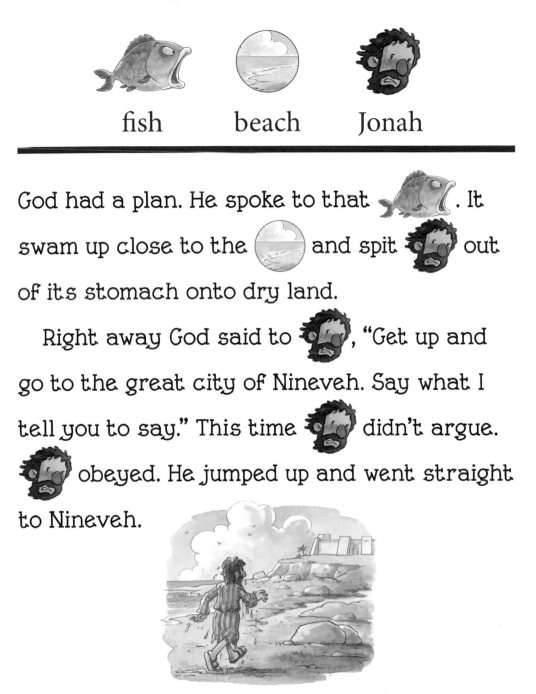. It swam up close to the and spit out of its stomach onto dry land.

Right away God said to , "Get up and go to the great city of Nineveh. Say what I tell you to say." This time didn't argue. obeyed. He jumped up and went straight to Nineveh.

New Testament Stories

An Angel's Message

122

Zechariah Gabriel baby

A priest named 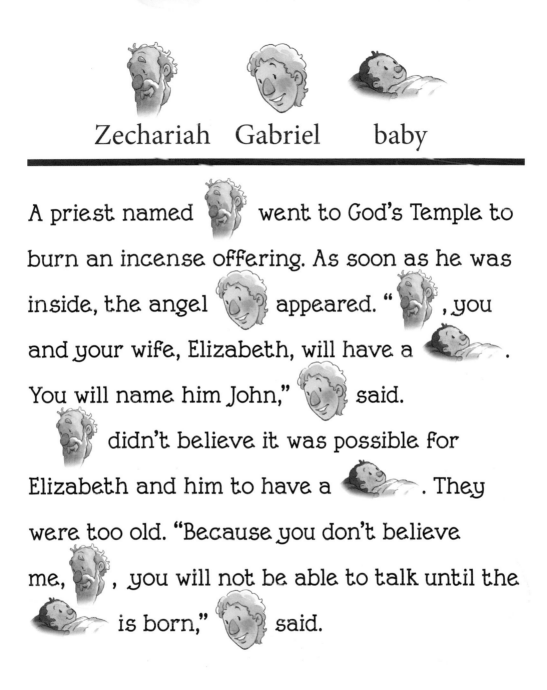 went to God's Temple to burn an incense offering. As soon as he was inside, the angel appeared. " , you and your wife, Elizabeth, will have a . You will name him John," said.

didn't believe it was possible for Elizabeth and him to have a . They were too old. "Because you don't believe me, , you will not be able to talk until the is born," said.

A Baby Named John

Luke 1:57–66

angel   baby   Zechariah

Just as the 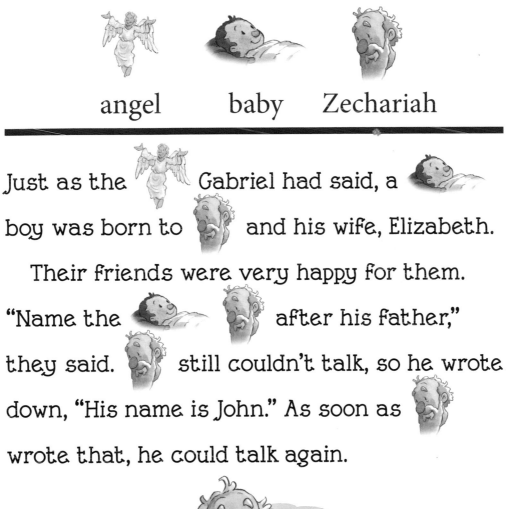 Gabriel had said, a

boy was born to and his wife, Elizabeth.

Their friends were very happy for them.

"Name the after his father,"

they said. still couldn't talk, so he wrote

down, "His name is John." As soon as

wrote that, he could talk again.

His name
is John.

Mary's Big Surprise

Luke 1:26–38

angel   Mary   baby

Not long after his visit to Zechariah, the angel Gabriel went to see a young woman named Mary. She was a cousin to Elizabeth, Zechariah's wife. Mary lived in Nazareth and was engaged to marry Joseph, a carpenter.

"Don't be afraid, Mary," the angel said. "God is pleased with you. You will have a baby and will name Him Jesus. He will be called the Son of God." This was a big surprise to Mary.

Joseph Marries Mary

Matthew 1:18–25

128

Joseph   baby   angel

When 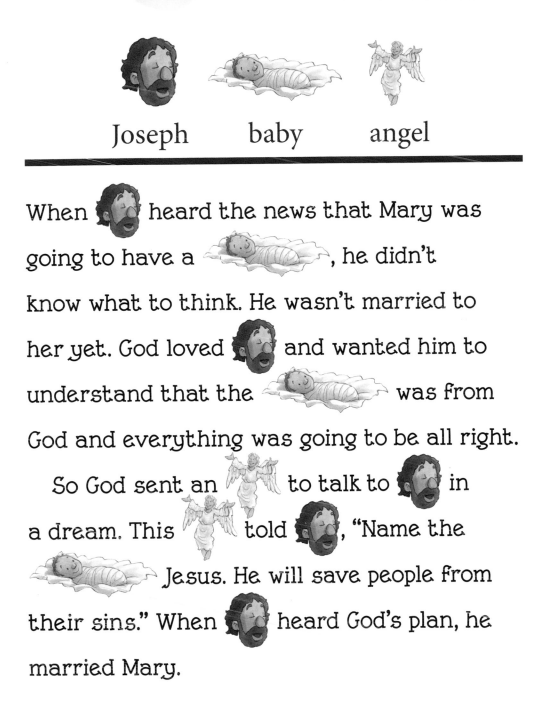 heard the news that Mary was going to have a baby, he didn't know what to think. He wasn't married to her yet. God loved Joseph and wanted him to understand that the baby was from God and everything was going to be all right.

So God sent an angel to talk to Joseph in a dream. This angel told Joseph, "Name the baby Jesus. He will save people from their sins." When Joseph heard God's plan, he married Mary.

God's Baby Son

Luke 2:1–7

people   animals   box

The ruler of the land, Augustus Caesar, made a new law to count all the . Everyone had to register in their hometown, so Joseph and Mary went to their hometown, Bethlehem. The town was full of . There was no place for Mary and Joseph to sleep.

Finally, Joseph found a place for them where the  were kept. And that's where God's baby Son, Jesus, was born. His first bed was on the hay in the  where the  were fed.

Some Sleepy Shepherds

Luke 2:8–12

shepherds   sheep   baby

That night, out in the fields, sleepy [shepherds] were taking care of their [sheep]. Suddenly an angel appeared in the sky. The angel's light was so bright, it hurt their eyes.

"Don't be afraid," the angel said. "I have good news for you. A [baby] was born in Bethlehem tonight. He is your Savior. You will find the [baby] lying in a feeding box."

What the Shepherds Saw

Luke 2:13–20

angels   shepherds   box

Then the whole sky filled up with so many , no one could count them all. They sang, "Glory to God in heaven!" And then, when the song was over, the  disappeared.

The  hurried to Bethlehem. They found Mary and Joseph and saw baby Jesus lying in the hay in the feeding . The  told them everything the  had said about the child.

Gifts for Baby Jesus

Matthew 2:1–12

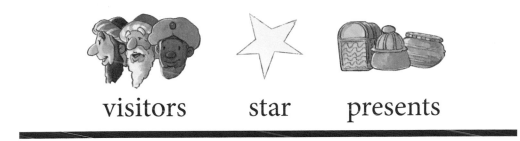

visitors   star   presents

Soon many of the people who came to register in Bethlehem went home. Mary and Joseph moved into a house.

One day they had 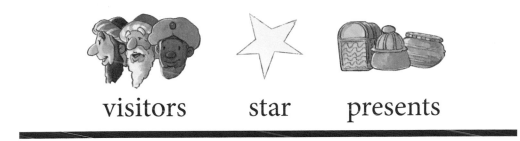 who came from far away in the east. These 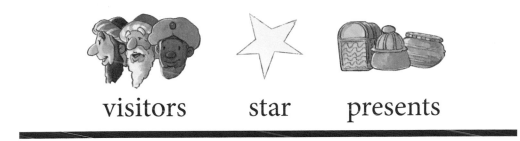 were wise men. They had followed a bright 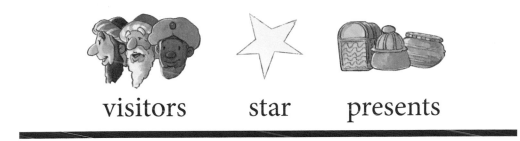 to find little Jesus. The 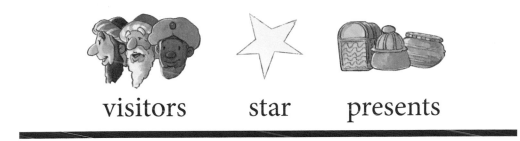 bowed down, worshipped God's only Son, and gave Him expensive 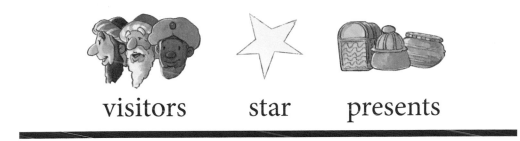 of gold, frankincense, and myrrh.

The Man Who Ate Locusts

Matthew 3:1–13; Mark 1:4–9

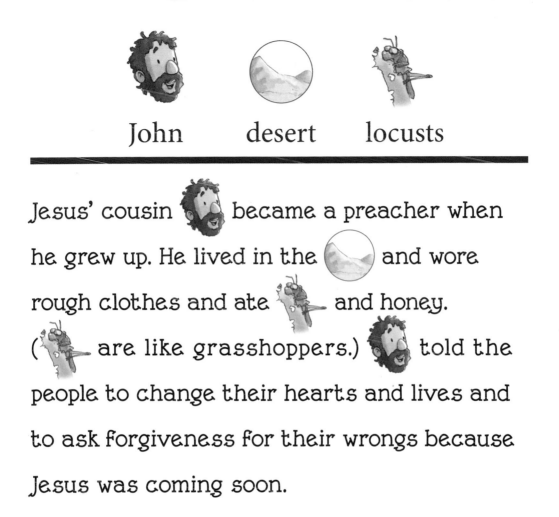

John   desert   locusts

Jesus' cousin became a preacher when he grew up. He lived in the and wore rough clothes and ate and honey. (are like grasshoppers.) told the people to change their hearts and lives and to ask forgiveness for their wrongs because Jesus was coming soon.

One day when Jesus was grown up, too, He went to the place where was preaching and baptizing people. Jesus asked to baptize Him in the river.

John Baptizes Jesus

Matthew 3:13–17

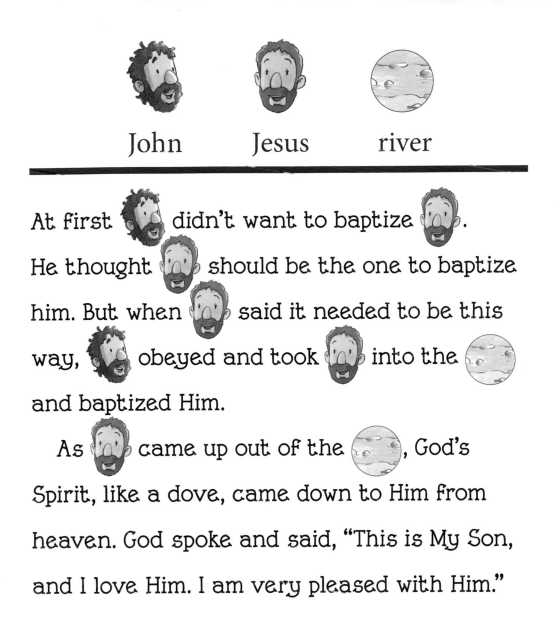

John   Jesus   river

At first John didn't want to baptize Jesus.

He thought Jesus should be the one to baptize

him. But when Jesus said it needed to be this

way, John obeyed and took Jesus into the river

and baptized Him.

As Jesus came up out of the river, God's

Spirit, like a dove, came down to Him from

heaven. God spoke and said, "This is My Son,

and I love Him. I am very pleased with Him."

A Little Boy Helps Jesus

John 6:1–13

people   fish   food

Great crowds of  followed Jesus to see His miracles and hear Him teach about God's love for them. One day a huge crowd of five thousand men and their families followed Jesus. It was late in the day, and the  were getting hungry.

A little boy gave Jesus five small loaves of bread and two . Jesus blessed the . His helpers gave it to the . After everyone had plenty to eat, the followers gathered up twelve baskets of leftover .

143

Jesus Stops a Storm

Mark 4:35–41

144

boat   lake   waves

Jesus and His followers got into a 🚢 and set out across the 🌅. Jesus was so tired that He fell asleep. Soon a strong wind began to blow. 🌊 came over the side of the 🚢. Everyone was very frightened.

They woke Jesus. "Help us, or we'll drown!" Jesus commanded the 🌊 and wind to be still. The wind stopped, and there were no more 🌊 coming into the 🚢. The 🌅 became calm.

A Very Poor Woman

Mark 12:41–44

money   box   woman

Jesus was watching people put their  into the collection  at the Temple where God's people worshipped. Some rich people were very proud as they put in a lot of .

Then a very poor  came. In the  went her two small coins. *Plunk! Plunk!* Jesus told His closest followers, "This  gave more than the rich people with many coins. The rich people gave only what they did not need, but this poor  gave all the  she had."

One Lost Sheep

Luke 15:3-7

Jesus   man   sheep

Here is a story Jesus told. A man had one hundred sheep, but he lost one. Now, what was the man going to do? He left his ninety-nine sheep safe at home and went looking for the one lost sheep.

The man searched everywhere, and when he finally found the lost sheep, he was so happy. The man put the sheep on his shoulders and carried it home.

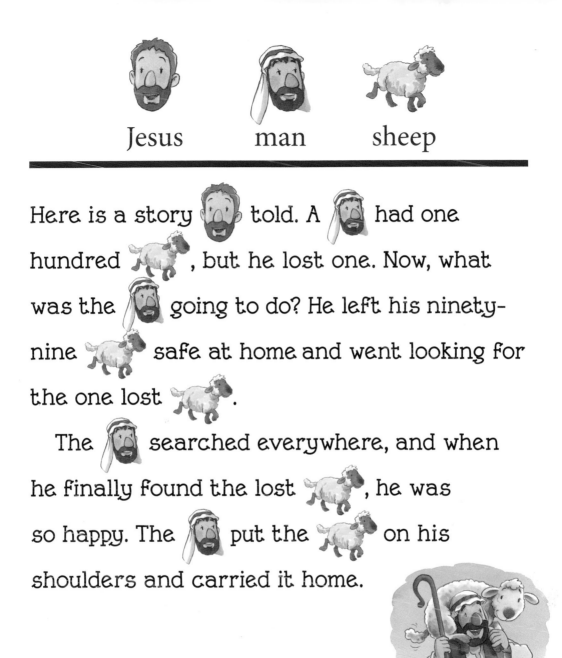

The First Lord's Supper

Matthew 26:26–29; 1 Corinthians 11:23–25

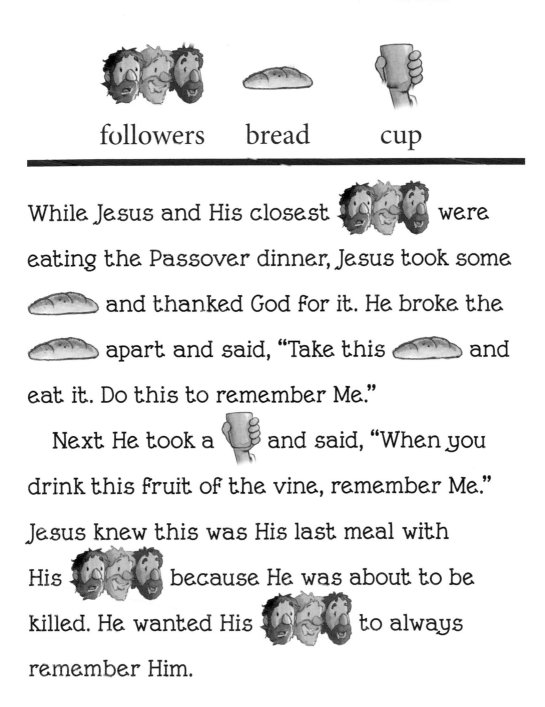

followers bread cup

While Jesus and His closest [followers] were eating the Passover dinner, Jesus took some [bread] and thanked God for it. He broke the [bread] apart and said, "Take this [bread] and eat it. Do this to remember Me."

Next He took a [cup] and said, "When you drink this fruit of the vine, remember Me." Jesus knew this was His last meal with His [followers] because He was about to be killed. He wanted His [followers] to always remember Him.

Jesus Prays for Help

Matthew 26:36–40; Mark 14:32–42; Luke 22:39–46

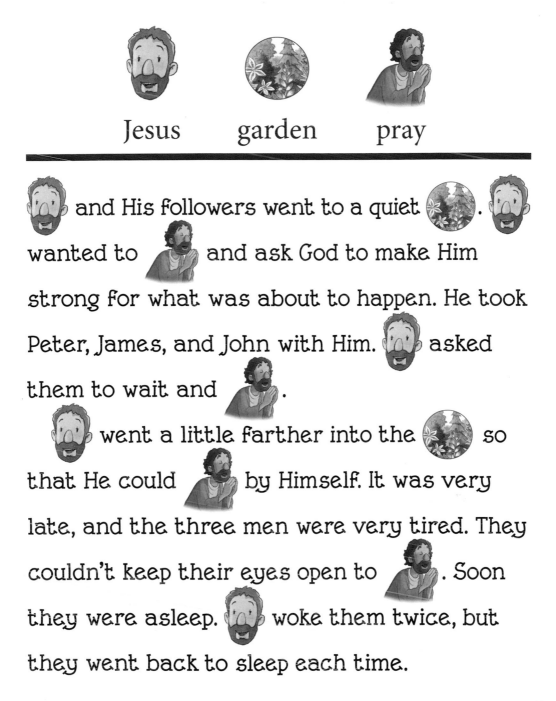

Jesus   garden   pray

and His followers went to a quiet . wanted to and ask God to make Him strong for what was about to happen. He took Peter, James, and John with Him. asked them to wait and .

went a little farther into the so that He could by Himself. It was very late, and the three men were very tired. They couldn't keep their eyes open to . Soon they were asleep. woke them twice, but they went back to sleep each time.

Jesus Is Arrested

Matthew 26:45–56; Luke 22:45–51; John 18:10–11

followers　　　sword　　　ear

The third time Jesus woke His , He said, "We must go. Here comes the man who has turned against Me." Just then a big crowd carrying torches and clubs came into the garden. Judas, one of Jesus' , was with them. He kissed Jesus on the cheek. It was a signal to the guards to arrest Jesus.

Peter pulled out his  and cut off the  of one guard. Jesus told Peter to put the  away. Then He healed the guard's .

Pilate Questions Jesus

Luke 22:52–23:25

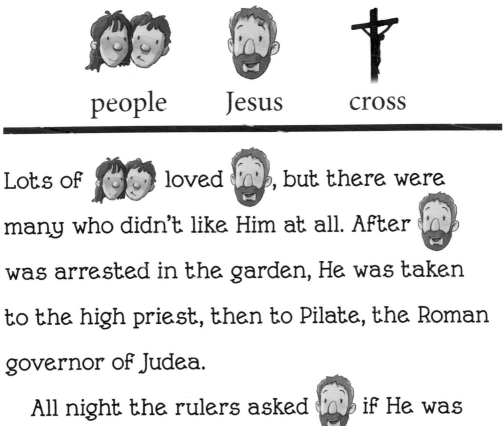

people   Jesus   cross

Lots of people loved Jesus, but there were many who didn't like Him at all. After Jesus was arrested in the garden, He was taken to the high priest, then to Pilate, the Roman governor of Judea.

All night the rulers asked Jesus if He was God's Son. They did not believe that He was. Finally Pilate said that he didn't think Jesus was guilty. But the people who hated Jesus kept yelling until Pilate decided that Jesus had to die on a cross.

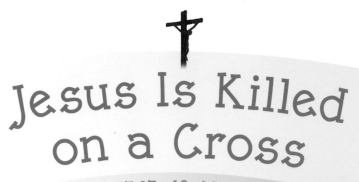

Jesus Is Killed on a Cross

Matthew 27:27–40; Mark 15:25–27

158

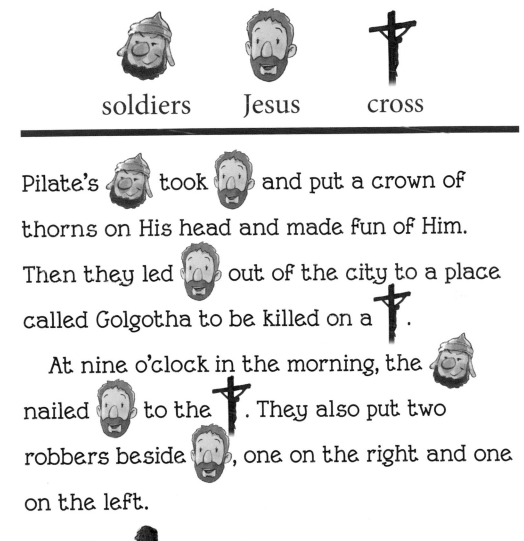

soldiers   Jesus   cross

Pilate's took and put a crown of thorns on His head and made fun of Him. Then they led out of the city to a place called Golgotha to be killed on a .

At nine o'clock in the morning, the nailed to the . They also put two robbers beside , one on the right and one on the left.

A Dark Day

Matthew 27:45–54; Luke 23:44–49; Hebrews 9

Jesus   cross   earthquake

While  was on the ✝, the land became dark from noon until three o'clock. Then  died, and there was a big  .

When the earth shook, the thick curtain in the Temple ripped from top to bottom. Now people could see inside the Most Holy Place. Before, only the High Priest got to see inside.

When the soldiers at the ✝ saw what happened when  died, they knew He really was the Son of God!

Jesus Is Laid in a Tomb

Luke 23:50–56

tomb   cross   stone

A rich man, named Joseph of Arimathea, had a new  where he had planned to be buried one day. He took Jesus' body from the  and put it in his own empty .

Joseph and Jesus' friends wrapped His body in strips of linen and laid it carefully in the . Roman soldiers came to guard the . They rolled a huge  in front of the door and sealed it in a way that would show if anyone tried to move the .

A Big Surprise

Matthew 28:1–10

women   stone   angel

The day after Jesus was buried was a holy day, so His friends had to stay home. Then very early on Sunday morning, the  went back to the tomb. It was the third day since Jesus died.

When the  got there, they couldn't believe their eyes. The  had been rolled away! An  of God was sitting on the ! The soldiers were so frightened, they were like dead men.

Jesus Is Alive!

Matthew 28:5–8; Luke 24:9–12

angel   women   friends

The  said, "Don't be afraid. Jesus is alive." Those  were as happy as they could be! They ran to find other  of Jesus.

Some of Jesus'  didn't believe what the  said. But everything the  said was true. Jesus was alive! He had risen from death.

Jesus Appears to a Room Full of Friends

Luke 24:36–49

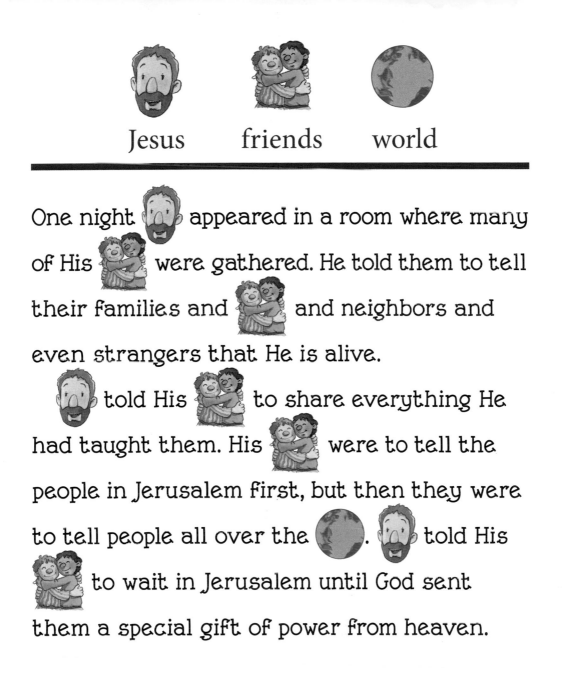

Jesus   friends   world

One night Jesus appeared in a room where many of His friends were gathered. He told them to tell their families and friends and neighbors and even strangers that He is alive.

Jesus told His friends to share everything He had taught them. His friends were to tell the people in Jerusalem first, but then they were to tell people all over the world. Jesus told His friends to wait in Jerusalem until God sent them a special gift of power from heaven.

Jesus Goes to Heaven

Luke 24:50–53; Acts 1:6–11

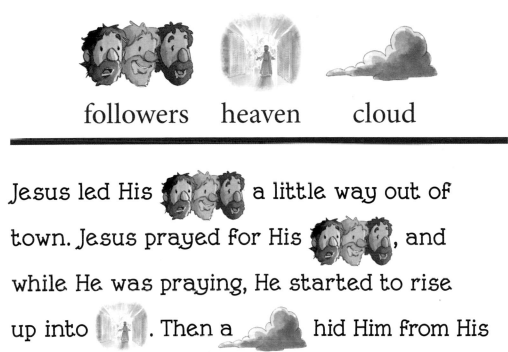

followers   heaven   cloud

Jesus led His a little way out of town. Jesus prayed for His , and while He was praying, He started to rise up into . Then a hid Him from His .

As everyone was standing there staring up into , two angels appeared beside the and said, "Jesus has been taken away from you and into . He will come back in the clouds, just like He went away."

God's Spirit Comes to Help

Acts 2:1–4

heaven   followers   fire

After Jesus went back to , His  were praying together in a big room. Suddenly something amazing happened.

First it sounded as if a huge wind were blowing. Next flames of  flickered over every person's head. Then God's Spirit came, and the  began to speak in different languages. This was the gift from God that Jesus had promised His .

A Mean Man

Acts 9:1–4

Jesus   Saul   light

There was a mean man chasing after followers of . His name was . He was sure that everything he heard about  was wrong.  didn't believe any of it. He was sure he was right. So  hurt, and even killed, people who believed in .

Well, God wanted  to work for Him. So one day when  was on a journey, God sent a bright flash of . The  was so bright,  fell to the ground.

Saul Is Blinded

Acts 9:4–9

Saul light city

"! Why are you doing things against Me?" a voice said from inside the .

"Who are You?" asked .

"I am Jesus. Now get up and go into the ."

When stood up, he was blind. His friends had to lead him into the .

 didn't eat or drink anything for three days.

Ananias Helps Saul

Acts 9:10–18; 13:9

Saul   pray   Jesus

God sent a man named Ananias to find 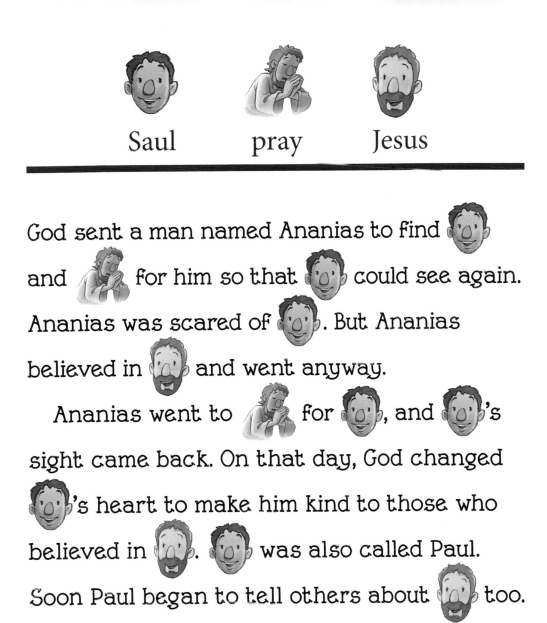 and 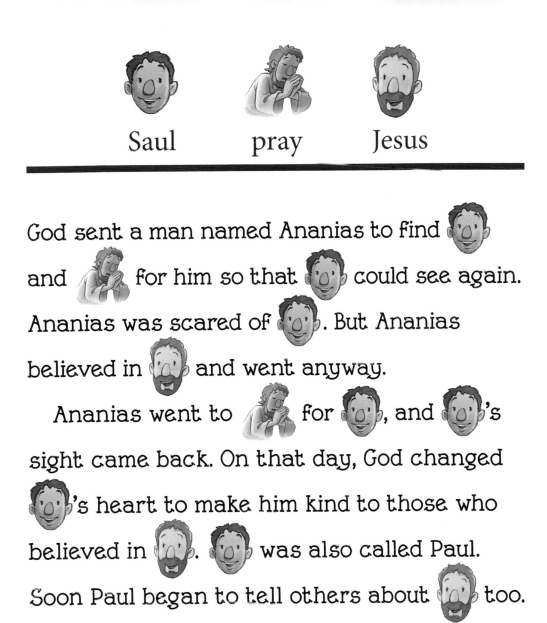 for him so that 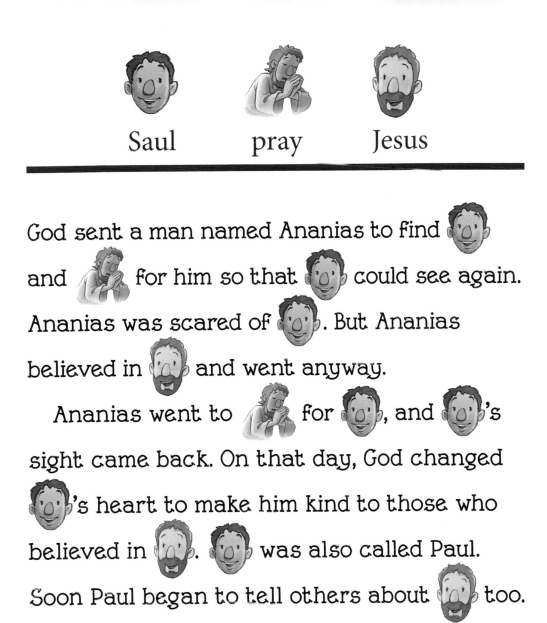 could see again. Ananias was scared of 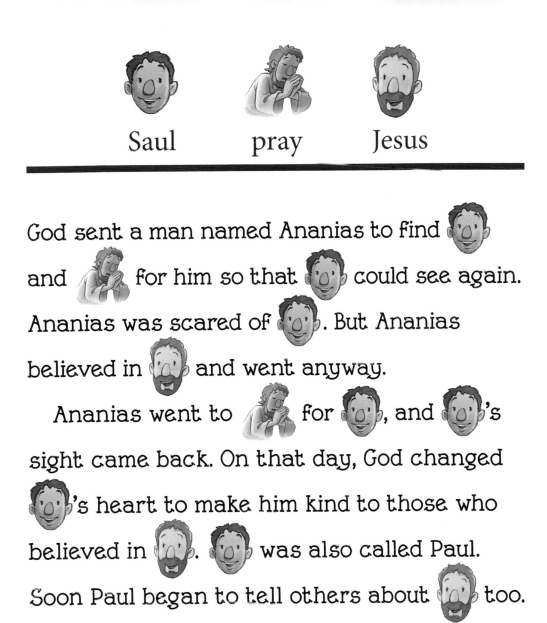. But Ananias believed in 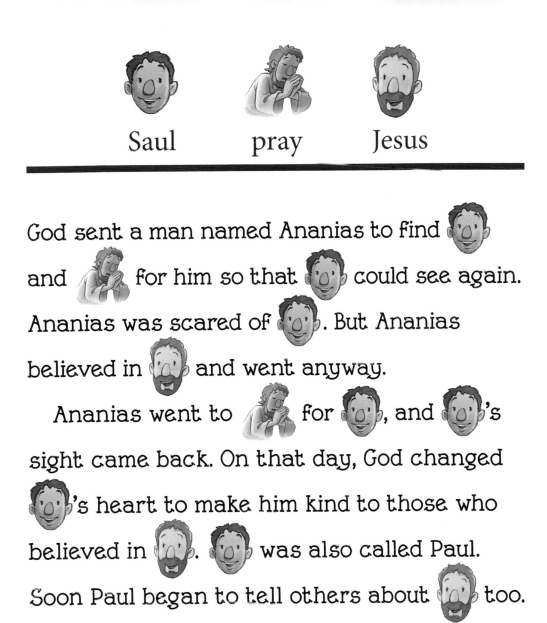 and went anyway.

Ananias went to 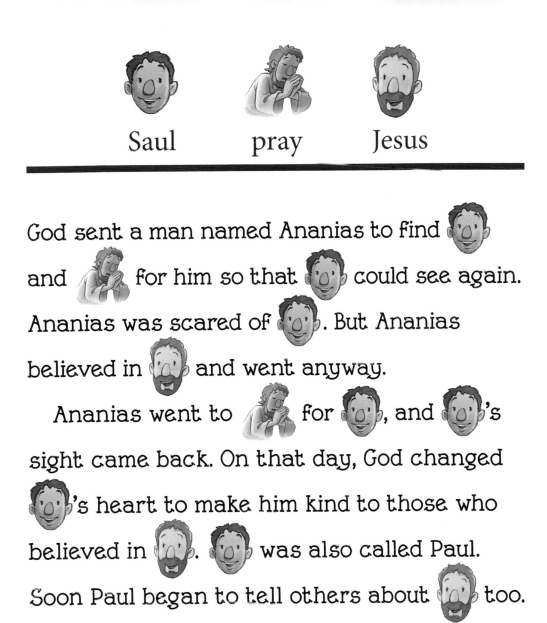 for 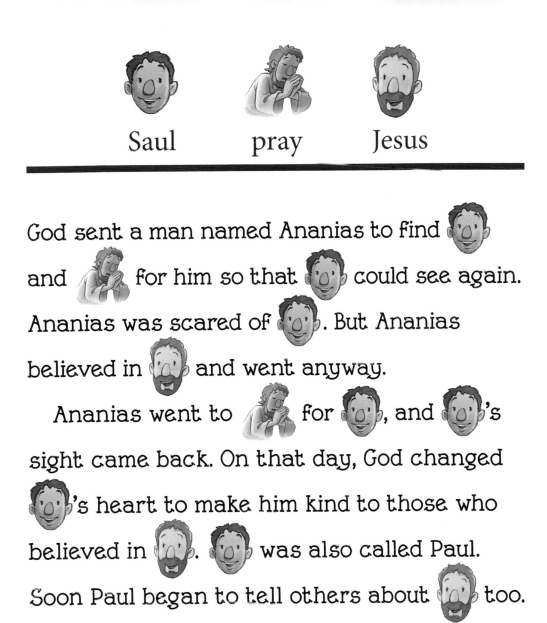, and 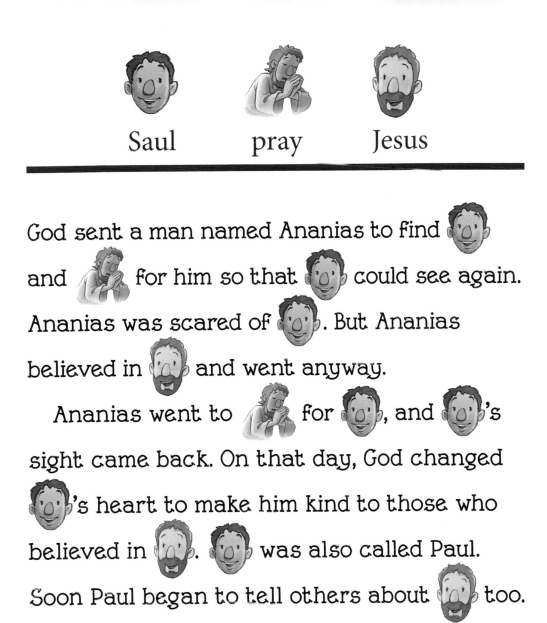's sight came back. On that day, God changed 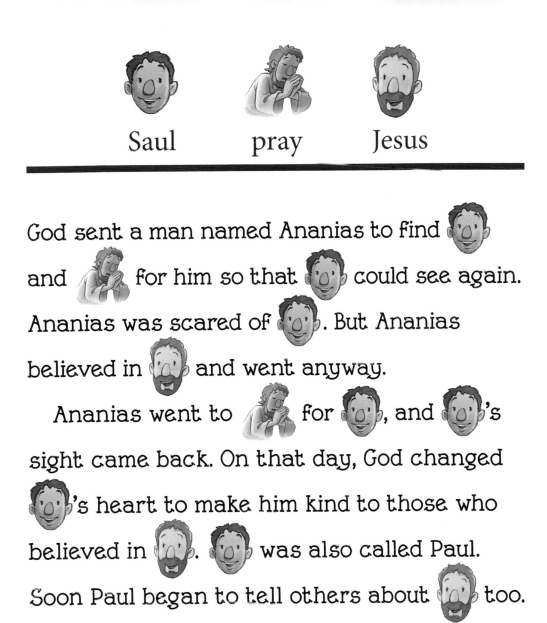's heart to make him kind to those who believed in 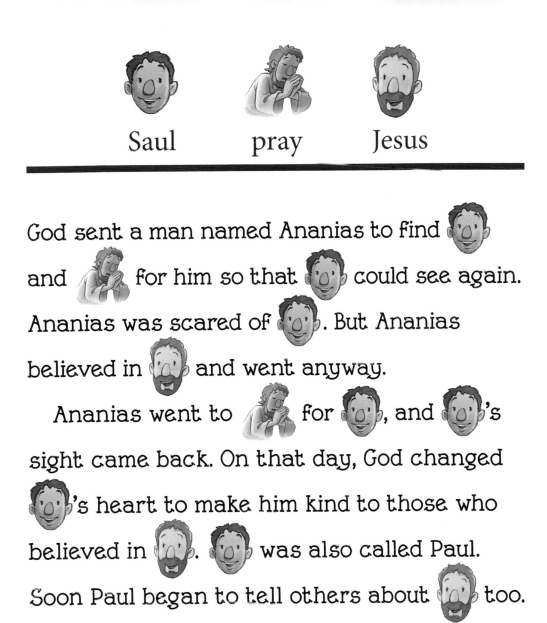. 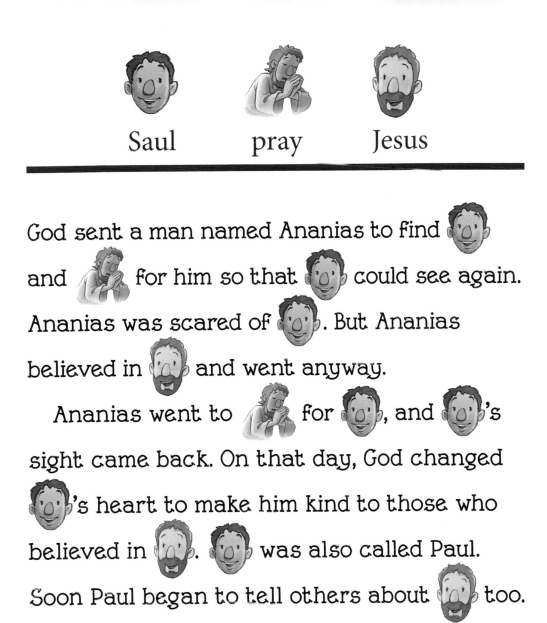 was also called Paul. Soon Paul began to tell others about 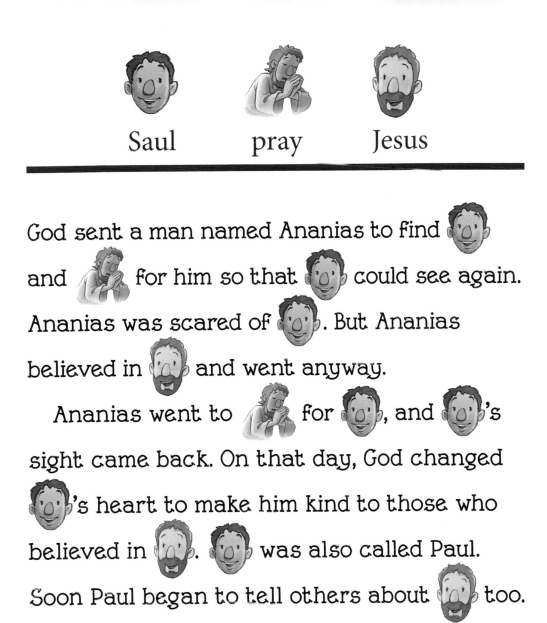 too.

Peter in Jail

Acts 12:1–18

Peter   jail   angel

One day King Herod threw 🖼, one of Jesus' followers, in 🖼. The king had sixteen soldiers guard 🖼 so he couldn't get away. That night an 🖼 came into 🖼's cell. "Hurry! Get up!" the 🖼 said. "Follow me." 🖼 thought he must be dreaming . . . but he wasn't. The chains fell off 🖼's hands, and the 🖼 led him past the guards. When they came to the iron gate of the 🖼, it swung open on its own, and 🖼 was free.

New Heaven and Earth

Revelation 21

heaven   earth   Jesus

One of the biggest promises God made was that we will live with Him in  forever. He said that there would be a new  and a new  and we would get a new body—one that won't get old but will live forever.

In the new , no one will ever be sad again. No one will ever die again. The streets will be made of gold, and there will be gates of pearl. Everything will be more beautiful than anything you can imagine. And best of all,  will be there. We will be with Him forever.

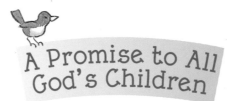

A Promise to All God's Children

"No one has ever seen this.
No one has ever heard about it.
No one has ever imagined
what God has prepared
for those who love him."

1 Corinthians 2:9